Side Effects May Include Happiness

HOW TO TRADE
YOUR 9-TO-5 MISERY
FOR YOUR LIFE'S PASSION

PARVIZ FIROUZGAR

Side Effects May Include Happiness –
How to Trade Your 9-to-5 Misery For Your Life's Passion
By Parviz Firouzgar

Cover Design by Melody Hunter

ISBN: 978-1-944177-61-4 (P)
ISBN: 978-1-944177-62-1 (E)

Crescendo Publishing, LLC
300 Carlsbad Village Drive
Ste. 108A, #443
Carlsbad, California 92008-2999
1 (877) 575-8814

www.CrescendoPublishing.com
GetPublished@CrescendoPublishing.com

Our deepest fear is not that we are inadequate.

Our deepest fear is that we are powerful beyond measure.

It is our light, not our darkness that most frightens us.

We ask ourselves, who am I to be brilliant,

gorgeous, talented and fabulous?

Actually, who are we not to be?

You are a child of God.

Your playing small doesn't serve the world.

There is nothing enlightened about shrinking
so that other people won't feel insecure around you.

We were born to make manifest the glory of God within us.

It is not just in some of us; it's in everyone.

As we let our own light shine, we unconsciously

give other people permission to do the same.

As we are liberated from our fear,
our presence automatically liberates others.

*- Taken from the 1994 inaugural
speech of Nelson Mandela*

A Message from the Author

Download a complimentary BONUS chapter here:

http://www.SuccessLibrary.com

What people are saying about *"Side Effects May Include Happiness"*

"Parviz is a brilliant teacher and businessman. The lessons he provides in **Side Effects May Include Happiness** are requirements for success in business. Not only does Parviz explain key business concepts but he also walks you through the action steps to apply them immediately to your business. This book should be required reading for all entrepreneurs."

–Nicole Carpenter
Entrepreneur & Author of
"A Heart Without A Home"

"This is a phenomenal book and it will change many lives. **Side Effects May Include Happiness** should be must read for all high school and college students. The lessons in this book will set the foundation to build a successful business. The chapter on our conscious and subconscious abilities is so powerful. The lesson on goals is amazing. I'm now also clear on my mission based on the questions Parviz asked in the chapter about motivation and the power of passion. After reading the chapter on raising capital I finally get it. Now I know how to 'attract' the money for my business. Thank you for writing this amazing book. I know it will impact many people."

–Chella Diaz
Founder of Money IQ

"This book is an incredible read. It teaches you the right mindset and attitude to have in order to achieve your dreams and goals. I love how it breaks down how to overcome your obstacles in order to achieve success in all areas of business and your life. I have implemented these effective tips on how to overcome what is holding me back from achieving my highest potential and I am already seeing a drastic difference in my performance and major improvement in my life. I highly recommend this book to those who have big goals and are determined to reach their highest potential."

–Sarah Johnson
Entrepreneur

"A very easy and enjoyably comprehensive read of a very important topic. It gets to the core of our creative freedoms and potential. A most definitive outline of our pursuit of happiness!"

–Bradley Warren Fox
Actor, Musician

"Still waiting until you're rich to be truly happy? What if there was a guidebook to show you how living your passion and becoming fulfilled will actually get you the money you so desire? *Side Effects May Include Happiness* is that guidebook, with the keys to success outlined in a quick and easy read. This book is like a modern-day *Think and Grow Rich*, with all the principles for happiness and success laid out right in front of you. If you're ready for happiness — and the money that can follow — read this book!"

–Jason Niedle
President, Tethos Creative
Adjunct Professor, Chapman University

"After reading Parviz's new book *Side Effects May Include Happiness*, it is very apparent that Parviz speaks from years and years of experience being a true Entrepreneur. Following his advice and his words of wisdom will send you down a path of success no matter what business you are involved in. A must read!"

–Robb Wood
Entrepreneur

"This is the book every beginning entrepreneur NEEDS to read before starting a business. As a student who wants to become an entrepreneur, this information took the mystery and fear out of it for me. It is a quick read filled with lessons that reveal the hidden genius inside each of our passions."

–Emily Rosca
Student

"**Side Effects May Include Happiness** lays out the guiding principles for a successful and fulfilling entrepreneurial journey. Focusing on inherent passions and outlining the traits and habits required, all entrepreneurs will find amazing value in this book. As an aspiring entrepreneur, I will absolutely be asking myself if I'm following Parviz's principles as I make business decisions going forward."

–Andrea Repp
Founder, Rendered Nest

Table of Contents

Introduction

How many people do you know, including yourself, who live a nine-to-five lifestyle and are genuinely happy? When I say "happy," I do not mean someone who just has fun on weekends. I am referring to those who feel fulfilled, who know that they are living the life they always dreamed of and were meant to live. I would guess you don't know many. Neither do I.

How about you? Are *you* living your purpose? Even if you don't conclusively know what your purpose is, deep down you know whether your life turned out the way you dreamed it would. If not, then your life is likely the result of conformity and having been pushed into the direction you took by your family, friends, and society in general. Most people fall into that category.

The overwhelming vast majority of people follow a life path of working for someone and then starting a family with a comfortable retirement down the line as their major goal. If they are middle class or (increasingly rarely) upper middle class, then society considers them to have become successful. But are they happy and fulfilled? Hardly. If you ask them if they are, they will frequently respond that they know they did not pursue their dreams but they now have comfort and security. It was a compromise worth making because their dreams involved too much risk.

But do they really have the level of security they think they do, working for someone else? Let's examine this massive misconception. First of all, the entire concept of lifetime employment with a secure retirement has become an ancient relic. It all but disappeared when increasing competition, especially from low-wage countries abroad, required employers to take cost-cutting measures just to stay in business.

Most people will remind you of a guaranteed paycheck, secure benefits, and vacations. Really? If you work for someone else, who controls your paycheck? Not you. It can be taken away at any time. Who controls your employment? Also not you. Your job can disappear in the blink of an eye for any number of reasons. In fact, in many states your employer doesn't even have to have a reason for firing you. These are called "at will" states, like California.

Who determines when you get a raise, when you are able to take a few weeks off for vacation, what level of benefits you receive, when you can retire, or anything else for that matter? It's definitely not you. Your employer controls every aspect of your employment and income. Every ingredient can be withheld or completely withdrawn at any time — and you will have no choice in the matter. Even if you are on great terms with your employer, market forces can easily override his desire to keep you on board or give you the benefits he wants to give you.

The life of a self-employed person is entirely different. Assuming their business is successful, then they control it all — their employment security, paycheck, raises, vacations, benefits, retirement, etc. All of it. They really do have security because they have control. Control is security. In order to obtain all of this, they need only the knowledge of how to become successful. With that, their life suddenly comes under their control and not someone else's.

So what does it take to get this knowledge? What does it take to become successful? And most important of all, can success become a predetermined certainty so that taking the plunge into entrepreneurship does not turn into a greater risk than working for someone else?

First, let's define success. My definition of success is doing what you love and making a good living doing it, which leads to a feeling of fulfillment — that is, a sense that you are living your purpose and enjoying every minute of it. It is a feeling you have in the depths of your soul, and it is entirely different from the superficial happiness that comes from having fun at your friend's latest party. Living a fulfilling life is real happiness.

Success is not about money. If you become successful in the way I just described, then the money will automatically follow. Trust me on this as I have experienced it multiple times. Even if it does not automatically follow, then there are ways to make it follow; I know as I have learned how to turn any viable business idea into an economic powerhouse. I describe these methods in my book *The Secrets of Wealth*. It is a book about how money accumulates according to certain timeless financial principles, but there is also a chapter in it that describes how these same financial principles can be injected into any business — for spectacular results. This knowledge empowers you to turn a business that is not doing great, albeit one you enjoy, into one that can make millions.

The following statement is of utmost importance and you need to take it to heart: *Money alone does not make you happy, successful, or grant you fulfillment.* We all know rich people who are miserable as can be because all they care about is making more money. The truth is they are not living their true passion. They have been misguided into an erroneous belief system where financial riches, material goods, and outdoing their neighbors and friends are their only goals.

Money is a by-product of success and fulfillment that can grant you much enjoyment, and yes, it can even buy you health. How else would you afford expensive medical care when you need it? Money is a powerful tool that can be used for great good in so many ways. However, having money alone pales beside what your life could be like if you did something you loved, especially when you add the joy of benefitting others as much as it may benefit you.

To quote a line from a Talking Heads song, "How did we get here?" Why are most of us swimming in a sea of mediocrity when only a few of us seem to have the Midas touch? These select few individuals live in a rarified atmosphere of repeated successes and affluence, all while doing what they truly love to do. How are they different? What do they know that we don't? *Most importantly, how is it possible that no matter what they set their minds to, their success is always a predetermined certainty?* Nothing is left to chance. Imagine if you were one of them!

Have you been cheated? No, you have not been cheated. You probably just never knew that this information is actually not that hard to find. You simply need to want to find the answers, and you need to know where to look. Additionally, you were not taught the right lessons because the people surrounding you didn't know them either. That is, they were also never shown how success can be a learned skill that almost anyone can master. It's a big problem with a surprisingly simple solution: search, find, learn, and then do it.

As they say, when the student is ready, the teacher will appear. Are you ready? If you are, then I am ready to be that teacher who can change your life for the better in ways you cannot even imagine right now. All the lessons you need to take control of your life and to become successful, fulfilled, and even wealthy are straight ahead.

The key is having the right knowledge. Knowledge is the currency of the universe. In our case it is a currency that can be converted into fulfillment, true happiness, and countless dollars as a by-product. With the right knowledge you will find out that you *can* live your dream. With the right knowledge you *can* do what you love and make a great living doing it. And yes, you *can* learn the right skills that will then take 99 percent of the risk out of the equation. Best of all, you will know in advance that you will succeed. Success *can* become a predetermined certainty for you — if you have a burning desire to learn, are ready to learn, are ready to accept that you do not know everything, and are teachable. Thereafter, all you have to do is act on the knowledge I will share with you.

The choice is yours. Know that if I can do it, so can you.

This book will teach you how to escape the shackles of a nine-to-five, paycheck-to-paycheck existence and live your dreams and passions — without the possibility of failure. Some of the lessons I will describe for you are also contained in my other books on entrepreneurship, such as my two *20/20 Hindsight* books plus my book on motivation — but there is a difference. This book contains only the lessons that you absolutely cannot do without — the mandatory lessons for becoming successful.

If you read the lessons in my other books that are not contained in this book, you will strengthen your potential even more as they are lessons that will keep you from making mistakes along the way. This brings up an important point.

Know that there is nothing wrong with making mistakes along the way. It is how we learn. It is how I learned. The distinction between the lessons I included and the ones I did not include in this book is this: If it is a lesson to avoid a potential mistake that would destroy your path to success, it is included in this book. If, on the other hand, it is a lesson that simply helps you avoid a temporary setback, the kind that all entrepreneurs experience, it may not be included here, but you will find it in my other books. Knowing about these ahead of time will simply accelerate your trajectory toward success and freedom. They will also save you time and money. In a nutshell, the *required* lessons — that is, those you *must* follow to become successful — will all be in the road map that is this book.

You may wonder how these lessons apply to your particular passion or dream. The truth is that the important lessons are universally transferrable to any business venture, and they are not technical skills. For example, if you want to open a chain of bakery stores because your passion is baking, lessons on baking are not included here. Baking would be considered a technical skill.

Technical skills are much less important, maybe 10 percent of the equation at best. You can always hire someone with the required technical skills for your business if you don't already have those skills, or you can take a course if you want to learn them for yourself. But the lessons that make all the difference apply to all businesses in all fields. Many of them are also life lessons, such as some required character traits and mind-sets that we'll discuss later. That's why this book is not filled with details on how to structure a corporation or how to do your company accounting. Those skills are similar to technical skills that you can learn along the way. In most cases the answer you need to resolve such issues is only a phone call away.

It is interesting to note that many people have a misconception regarding the importance — or lack of importance — of technical skills. This misconception is very wisely outlined in Michael E. Gerber's groundbreaking book *The E-Myth* (which stands for *The Entrepreneurial Myth*). He outlines how many people with great technical skills believe they can start their own business. After all, they have better technical skills than their bosses or even the owners of the company, so why shouldn't they become their own boss and run the show?

This misconception inevitably leads to disaster, as the "technician" does not have the required business skills to operate a successful business in his field — or any other. Nonetheless, if his previous employer was a great businessman and therefore made his job look easy, this misconception becomes understandable.

When an individual who possesses great technical skills but lacks important business skills enters the entrepreneurial workspace, they find themselves in a very precarious position. They end up working substantially more hours than they did as an employee and earning substantially less money because they don't know how to build and run a successful business. Skills that lead to success are completely separate from technical skills, and one is infinitely more important than the other.

This situation almost always leads to deep disappointment and sometimes total financial disaster. All the "technician" has done is create a job for themselves with less pay and more work. Independence, success, wealth, and freedom remain a distant dream.

So do not be concerned with what you want to do. It doesn't matter. The lessons you need to learn apply to all types of business activities. In fact, they also apply to basically any country in the free world. This means that these lessons apply not just to what you do but also where you do it. For example, if you wanted to open a business in Europe but didn't know their particular rules, regulations, and bureaucratic requirements, all you'd need to do is bring someone on board from your country of choice to handle that side of it. His duties are like those of a technician, available for you to hire. All the important success-oriented lessons that you are about to learn would apply there as much as they would apply in your hometown.

Here's an analogy of some of the benefits you will experience by moving from being a mere spectator to actually participating and joining the ranks of the successful and wealthy elite.

Imagine a ten-meter diving board. When you stand at the bottom looking up, it looks very tall — because it is. You watch people jump off and you admire their courage. Should you try it? It would definitely be an admirable accomplishment that only a few people will ever fulfill, similar to taking the plunge into entrepreneurship.

You decide to climb up the long flight of steps to get a closer look from the top. The climb alone is daunting. A ten-meter diving board really is high. As you make your way to the top and eventually stand on the edge, an inevitably frightening realization suddenly appears: It looks *much* higher from the top looking down than it does from below looking up. It looks so high, in fact, that the pool below looks too small. It genuinely appears that you could easily jump too far forward and hit the concrete, causing instant death. So how do other people overcome their fears and even enjoy stepping into this rather lengthy free fall?

Experienced Olympic divers will actually do triple or quadruple flips with multiple twists off a ten-meter diving board and then enter the water headfirst with barely a splash. Amazing! But that's not what we're talking about here. We're simply contemplating stepping off the edge and falling feet first into the pool. Realistically, that's quite an accomplishment when it's your first time.

I vividly remember my first time doing this in a swimming pool in France right on the Swiss border when I was only about fourteen or fifteen years old. I lived in Switzerland at the time and regularly rode my bicycle across the border to meet friends at this public swimming pool. There was a one-meter, a three-meter, and a ten-meter diving board. As I stood on the top of the ten-meter board for the first time, I was gripped by fear. I wanted the accomplishment, but I was afraid. Before I made the climb, I'd been watching another teenager as he jumped off repeatedly with nothing but enjoyment in his expression. Fortunately, he gave me some advice on how to position my arms and legs so that they would not slap against the water. He also told me how to step off the edge so that I would land in the middle of the pool.

I decided I no longer wanted to be a mere spectator. I stepped off the ledge into the abyss below. The rush was incredible as I could clearly feel the enormous acceleration. I dropped into the water feet first and came out with a grin on my face that felt like it stretched from ear to ear.

In retrospect, the experience ended up being less scary than I thought it would be, and it wasn't all that difficult since I had received good guidance from a fellow jumper. I did it. And then I did it again and again until eventually I was able to give other first-time jumpers similar wise guidance.

It was the same when I parachuted the first (and only) time. After five hours of preparation that seemed to never end, after sitting on the cold floor of an airplane with the door open until we got to 13,000 feet above the California desert, and then after sitting on the edge looking down at the earth, which was so far below me that I could barely make out a few scattered buildings, I remember thinking "good day to die" and then falling forward into the unknown. It was a tandem jump, so I had an instructor strapped to my back, but that had little impact on my level of fear when, for some inexplicable reason, I decided to jump out of a perfectly good airplane.

Skydiving ended up being not only an awesome accomplishment in my life, but an unbelievably enjoyable experience. The exhilaration of seeing your parachute open above you and thereby knowing you're going to make it back to the ground alive is indescribable.

There was also a profound lesson in this experience that was really no different from the one I learned from jumping off a ten-meter diving board. The lesson carries over into any other endeavor, such as becoming an entrepreneur for the first time, which similarly carries a lot of initial trepidation with it.

Jumping into any kind of unknown, literally or figuratively, is an adventure that is always accompanied by initial fear storms. So how do people do it and come out surviving and even thriving on the other side? *They do it with the help of proper guidance and the knowledge that if other people can do it, they can too.*

That's the bottom line ... and that is your first lesson. You can do it, and in order to do it, you only need the guidance from someone who has already successfully done it, like my skydiving instructor who had jumped out of an airplane more than a 1,000 times and lived to tell about it. You need to follow that guidance, and you need to follow it without ever thinking that you know better. Remember that you don't know what you don't know.

The proper guidance in any adventure, whether it's jumping out of an airplane or opening your first business, will open up new worlds to you that you have simply never experienced before — and probably didn't even know were there. Let those who do know, from experience, guide you. Think about this: The only way to walk through a minefield is to walk in someone else's footsteps. How else would you navigate through such dangerous terrain without getting blown up? It is the same in any other endeavor, including entrepreneurship. Follow in the footsteps of those who have already done it.

The thirteenth-century Persian poet Rumi said, "When setting out on a journey, do not seek advice from those who have never left home."

The aforementioned discussion leads us to an interesting question: why do the vast majority of people get guided into a nine-to-five, paycheck-to-paycheck lifestyle? The reason is actually simple: We get our guidance from all the wrong people. As already mentioned, our guidance should come from people with experience. If you want to learn how to white-water raft, wouldn't you want to learn from someone who has done it for many years so that their experience can teach you how to stay safe and have fun at the same time? If you want to learn how to climb mountains, wouldn't you want to learn from someone who has climbed more than a hundred peaks and lived to tell about it?

So here's the dilemma: When seeking guidance on how to become successful or even wealthy, whom do most of us go to? First, we go to our parents, who are probably living a nine-to-five lifestyle themselves and have never experienced true success and wealth. Assuming they are open to guiding us toward our dreams and passions, which most parents are not, then from what experience do they speak? None.

Then we talk to our friends and acquaintances, most of who are in the same boat we are in and have no experience outside the world of conformity and compromise. Finally, we talk to guidance counselors who have never been self-employed and thus have zero experience in anything but more conformity, compromise, and mediocrity.

Some of us will then move on to business school, thinking that's where we will learn the lessons we need to follow our passion. But most business school lessons are nothing but theory that has little to no application in the real world, outside of working for a large corporation — and even that's debatable. To make matters worse, those business school lessons are taught by professors who have never worked outside the academic environment and therefore have no real-life experience in any kind of business whatsoever.

Do you see the problem?

Pitifully few people are living up to their full potential, which they can only do by following their purpose, and our purpose is embedded in our dreams and passions. It is how we were made, and it is the path we are meant to follow in order to achieve a life of fulfillment. It is the path God wants us to follow. Just as Nelson Mandela wisely said, "Your playing small doesn't serve the world."

You have it in you to reach for and achieve greatness, to live a life of accomplishment and prosperity, helping your fellow man in the process, following your passions and living your dreams. You only need to get the right guidance from people who know how it's done because they've been there and done that. Side effects *will* include happiness!

> *"The two most important days in your life are the day you are born and the day you find out why."*
>
> –Mark Twain

The lessons in the following pages are your road map to success. You could even call it your treasure map. Although there is no particular order to these lessons, the key is this: If you follow all the lessons, success will become a virtual certainty. If you neglect any one of them, you change the picture dramatically. With some exceptions, it does not make success impossible, but it will make it extremely difficult. The corners you will have to cut, such as compromising your integrity, are not ones you will be proud of in the end, nor will they help you in the long run. So my advice to you is this: Treat this road map like a jigsaw puzzle. If you leave out one of the pieces, the end result will not be complete, and the missing piece will be staring everyone who is watching in the face. Most importantly, your chances for success will be dramatically reduced.

As I mentioned, there are exceptions, but most of these lessons simply cannot be ignored. They are absolutes. You cannot succeed without them. So do yourself a favor and don't neglect any of them.

Before we get started, here's one other piece of advice: Although anyone who wants to become independent, successful, and even wealthy can do so, it is not for everyone. Not everyone is cut out to be an entrepreneur. Not everyone is willing to make the effort, and not everyone is driven in the same way most entrepreneurs are. For example, some people are just too lazy for the effort that's required, and some people just have the wrong mind-set for success. That's okay. If you find that it's not for you, don't beat yourself up over it.

The world needs people who are not entrepreneurs just as much as it does those who are. The reason is somewhat obvious. Consider a sales organization. Can salespeople function without administrative people to support the sales they make? No they cannot. Likewise, will administrative people have a job if there are no salespeople to make sales? Obviously not. They need each other. Many sales positions are quite similar to entrepreneurship, so the analogy is very accurate. Entrepreneurs need to be able to hire administrative employees. Administrative employees need jobs that often come from entrepreneurs. It is a symbiotic relationship we cannot do without.

So whatever side of the fence you're on, it's okay. If you know you were born to follow your passions and live your dreams, I will show you how to make them happen. If you don't yet know where you stand, you'll find out quickly as you continue reading.

"You can make a wish or you can make it happen."

The Power of Persistence

*"Nothing in this world can take
the place of persistence.
Talent will not; nothing is more common
than unsuccessful men with talent.
Genius will not; unrewarded genius
is almost a proverb.
Education will not; the world is
full of educated derelicts.
Persistence and determination alone are omnipotent."*

–Calvin Coolidge

As I was designing the structure of this book in my mind, my thoughts kept coming back to the issue of persistence and determination. This is a lesson that essentially can overshadow any other in the impact it can have on your ability to succeed at whatever you set your mind to. For this reason I will follow my intuition and lead with a discussion on persistence and determination. As usual, there is always more to it than meets the eye.

I am writing this chapter as a source of comfort to you because once you master the art of persistence, you have a weapon at your disposal that can overcome essentially any obstacle. Persistence comes from passion and motivation, topics that we will delve into in depth later.

Consider that almost any kind of substantial achievement throughout history always involved setbacks, roadblocks, apparently insurmountable obstacles, hardship, and/or adversaries trying to block innovation in support of their own interests. In every case these were always overcome by persistence and determination.

A glowing example of all the above wrapped up into one intrepid entrepreneur's journey to victory is that of William McGowan, CEO of MCI Communications. Following the filing of MCI's 1974 lawsuit against AT&T, McGowan's single-minded obsession eventually led to a 1982 agreement leading to the divestiture of AT&T and the opening of the long-distance telephone market to competition within the United States. Note that at the time AT&T was one of the largest and most influential and powerful companies in the world — and they fought back in any way they could, not wanting to give up any part of their monopoly. Nonetheless, one man's determination led to the breakup of "Ma Bell" and gave us the marketplace of multiple carriers that we know today.

This is a classic David versus Goliath story. History is filled with them, and they all have one common ingredient, the steadfast "failure is not an option" determination and persistence of a single individual. Bill McGowan grew MCI into an entity worth $9.5 billion in revenue that controlled 16 percent of the American domestic and international long-distance market.

In October 2008, *Entrepreneur* magazine said it like this:

> Time and again he was told that AT&T was simply too big and too powerful. But through a combination of dogged determination, hard work, and a healthy dose of chutzpah, McGowan shattered AT&T's monopoly, kicked open the door to free competition in the long-distance market, and transformed a

struggling company into the world's second-largest long-distance carrier.

Working for MCI Communications was my one and only venture into the corporate world. While there I had the pleasure of meeting Bill McGowan when he personally presented me with a sales award. I remember him being very enthusiastic and simply a charming man to be around.

Thomas Edison, inventor of the modern-day light bulb, is another example. He had no special advantage, like most entrepreneurs. In fact, his teachers said he was "too stupid to learn anything." He was fired from his first two jobs for being "non-productive." As an inventor, Edison made 10,000 unsuccessful attempts before he got it right and invented the light bulb. When a reporter asked him, "How did it feel to fail 10,000 times?" Edison replied, "I didn't fail 10,000 times. I simply found 10,000 ways how not to make a light bulb."

Whether it's Henry Ford, Walt Disney, Steve Jobs, Elon Musk, Bill Gates, or scores of other groundbreaking entrepreneurs, they all had determination and persistence as their number-one weapon to achieve their dream — and the same applies to the successful business owner down the street: the baker, the car dealer, or the health-food storeowner. It doesn't just apply to those individuals who change the course of history and create headline news stories with their inventions or accomplishments. It applies to every success story, large and small. It will apply to your success as well.

I made persistence and determination major ingredients in my entrepreneurial journey early on. To this day, fate tests me every time I start a new venture. The inevitable path I am always led down is this: I come up with an idea that interests me tremendously and has the potential to develop into a real passion, even if I know little to nothing about the industry. I dive right in without hesitation and start a company. As I start putting the pieces together, learn what I need to learn, and move forward, a seemingly insurmountable roadblock suddenly appears from out of nowhere. Everything looks like it's going to fall apart — but I push on.

I have never yet failed to come up with a solution to overcome the roadblock, and I accredit that to my own "failure is not an option" attitude. I persist, and the solution to the problem always appears from out of nowhere, just like the problem did in the first place. Granted, there is some method to this madness, as we will discuss later. It involves a problem-solving technique that repeatedly works miracles in the lives of anyone who knows how to use it.

There is more power built into a "failure is not an option" attitude than we realize. Consider that if we raised our children without thoughts of failure, then failure would not be an option in life for them. "Nothing is impossible" becomes their only reality. If failure is not an option, then failure is not an option. A fascinating analogy is that many native tribes did not know the concept of lying until white settlers forced it upon them. Hence it was never in their repertoire for resolving conflicts. The entire concept of lying was unknown to them — until we showed up.

What is the bottom-line benefit to being determined and persistent, other than just not giving up? It is overcoming failure. Failure and mistakes are not just part of every entrepreneur's journey, they are much, much more than that. They are one of the universe's greatest blessings.

I have learned to embrace my failures and mistakes. Not only have they increased my level of resiliency, but they have also taught me some of the most important lessons I have ever learned. In fact, the lessons we learn from our mistakes and failures are vastly more profound than those we learn from our successes.

Our first success actually becomes the foundation for failure, and for this reason you should pay close attention to what I'm about to tell you. Only then can you avoid this pitfall. When we succeed for the first time, we start to think we can do no wrong, and we believe it's going to last forever. Worse still, we often let our ego get out of control because we think we've learned it all and have become infallible. This typically leads to complacency in our business as our new image now takes precedence over continuing to grow our business. The resulting complacency is business death. A business can never stand still. It must always be innovating, improving, growing, and moving forward; otherwise, it will start moving backward as a competitor soon appears to occupy our previous space in the economic world.

The lessons we learn from our first business collapse are invaluable, and the most important one is humility. We are not infallible. It may not last forever. Our business cannot be neglected in favor of spending all our time enjoying our newfound affluence. If you want to avoid such a dramatic event, then develop humility now, not when failure forces you to. Never let your business just coast along. It will start sliding backward before you know it.

Most successful entrepreneurs, including myself, have had one or two dramatic failures in their initial journey, often losing everything overnight. The way to avoid having this happen to you is by following the advice I just gave you.

You will still make mistakes, and you may still experience an occasional failure, but they should never cause you to give up on your passions and your dreams. You must persist. The benefits of steadfast determination are exceptionally simple to comprehend if you think of them this way: To succeed, all you need to do is get up one more time than you fall down. Try hard enough and long enough, and success will become inevitable. How else can it be? As they say, if you flip a coin often enough, eventually it has to come up heads.

Here are a few more inspirational examples of individuals throughout history who did not give up despite enormous setbacks. We all know their legacy.

- As a young man, Abraham Lincoln went to war a captain and returned a private. Afterward, he was a failure as a businessman. As a lawyer in Springfield, he was too impractical and temperamental to be a success. He turned to politics and was defeated in his first try for the legislature, again defeated in his first attempt to be nominated for Congress, defeated in his application to be commissioner of the General Land Office, defeated in the senatorial election of 1854, defeated in his efforts for the vice presidency in 1856, and defeated in the senatorial election of 1858. At about that time, he wrote in a letter to a friend, "I am now the most miserable man living. If what I feel were equally distributed to the whole human family, there would not be one cheerful face on the earth."

- Winston Churchill repeated a grade during elementary school and, when he entered Harrow, was placed in the lowest division of the lowest class. Later, he twice failed the entrance exam to the Royal Military Academy at Sandhurst. He was defeated in his first effort to serve in Parliament. He became prime minister at the age of sixty-two. He later wrote: "Never give in, never give in, never, never, never, never — in nothing, great or small, large or petty — never give in except to convictions of honor and good sense. Never, Never, Never, Never give up."

- Sigmund Freud was booed from the podium when he first presented his ideas to the scientific community of Europe. He returned to his office and kept on writing.

- Albert Einstein did not speak until he was four years old and did not read until he was seven. His parents thought he was "sub-normal," and one of his teachers described him as "mentally slow, unsociable, and adrift forever in foolish dreams." He was expelled from school and was refused admittance to the Zurich Polytechnic School.

- Henry Ford failed and went broke five times before he succeeded.

- An expert said of Vince Lombardi: "He possesses minimal football knowledge and lacks motivation." Lombardi would later write: "It's not whether you get knocked down; it's whether you get back up."

As Calvin Coolidge said, "Persistence and determination alone are omnipotent." Nothing else compares, and as I already mentioned, it applies equally to the greatest minds in history as it does to the baker down the road.

> *"I don't believe I have special talents,*
> *I have persistence. ...*
> *After the first failure, second failure,*
> *third failure, I kept trying."*
>
> –Carlo Rubbia, Nobel Prize–winning physicist

NEVER GIVE UP!

"Never, never, never give up!"

Your Attitude Toward Success

"If you don't have the right mindset
for success, it's over.
If you don't have the right character
for success, it's over.
If you don't have the right habits for success, it's over."

−T. Harv Ecker, Personal growth expert

I refer to this lesson as a foundational requirement. If you don't find yourself like-minded with this chapter's requirements, you will have to either change your mindset or give up on the idea of entrepreneurship. If you are not like-minded with the required attitude toward success, then your chances of succeeding are essentially eliminated. Your attitude toward success as I will describe shortly is the foundation of all achievement for an entrepreneur who also wants to get wealthy.

This may also be the most controversial issue that we will cover in this book. It crosses over into political territory and will therefore always be a subject of intense debate and disagreement. Despite this, I am not here to debate the issue with you. You are entitled to your own opinions, but you are not entitled to your own facts. I am here to tell you how it is based on experience and observation of numerous individuals on both sides of the fence. This is one of those absolutes that cannot be violated.

You need to ask yourself a number of questions. The first is whether you believe that the majority of rich people made their money honestly or dishonestly. If you believe that the wealthy mostly made their money through dumb luck, inheritance, special favors, cheating, or dishonesty, then your chances of becoming wealthy yourself are close to nil. For one thing, you would be wrong. The truth is that the vast majority of wealthy people made their fortune through honest hard work and persistence, mostly in somewhat unexciting professions.

A great book was published in 1996 called *The Millionaire Next Door: The Surprising Secrets of America's Wealthy* by Thomas J. Stanley and William D. Danko. The book is a compilation of research done to define the majority of America's millionaires. The most interesting — and surprising — result is that many millionaires accumulated their fortunes by living below their means. Most of the millionaire households they profiled did not have the extravagant lifestyles most people would expect them to have. They actually spent very little on cars and luxuries, such as expensive suits, watches, and vacations, or on high-profile homes. In fact, in many cases you couldn't even tell they were millionaires just by observing them in their neighborhood or how they spent their money. There are countless families just like that, living a quiet, middle-class lifestyle although their net worth is in the millions.

What is also surprising is that the vast majority of millionaires do not work in high profile, exciting industries. Their professions usually contain an aspect of something they are very passionate about, but they are not all inventors of revolutionary products. Most of them are in very average industries that most of us would initially view as dull, as dull as making ball bearings.

Consider this for a moment: *Why do rich people stay rich and poor people stay poor? It is because rich people live like poor people, and poor people live like rich people.* Think about it. This saying is not intended to be taken literally, but the point should be obvious; and we should all integrate this point into our lives.

There are obviously notable exceptions to what I just told you regarding millionaires being mostly honest and hardworking individuals. This is witnessed by news stories detailing certain individuals and the scandals they create from making their money dishonestly — the Bernie Madoffs of the world. But although there's always one high-profile story of such a crook that grabs our attention, they are a small minority in the big picture.

Next, how do you view your economic standing in relation to society? Do you believe that the world has cheated you and therefore owes you something? Do you believe your government owes you a living? Are you always looking to get something for free, blame others for all your misfortunes, and frown upon the success of others, even trying to bring them down? If any of these apply to you, then your chances for success are also near zero. People with a welfare and dependency mentality, those who are always blaming others, cannot become successful. It is a virtual mathematical impossibility.

People with the potential to become successful take full responsibility for every aspect of their lives: past, present, and future. Successful people don't live in the past. The past is dead, and we cannot change it. They understand that we've all had challenges, hardships, bad breaks, and misfortune. It is part of life. They don't blame anyone, nor do they seek compensation from society. They understand that the right thing to do is accept responsibility for everything, as everything that manifests in our lives was somehow attracted into our lives by us, most often to teach us the lessons we needed to learn. That's just the way the world works.

Character plays into this chapter also. Your maximum chance for success is manifested if you are honest, humble, want to help others, and live your life with integrity, doing what's right for the sake of doing the right thing. The definition of "integrity" is doing the right thing when no one is watching. Do you do the right thing without the need for acknowledgement from others for your good deeds, or do you use moments when no one is watching to cheat your way into an unfair advantage? What you should know is that life is like a bed of snow, wherever you tread, *eventually* your tracks will show.

Personal responsibility will always separate the winners from the losers. Those that play the victim are only cheating themselves out of all that could be. This is one of those absolute laws of the universe we must learn, like what goes around comes around.

To help you understand how concrete and unchangeable these laws are, consider this: *"As you do unto others, it will be done unto you."* I know you've heard it before, but do you believe in it?

Now here's the irony: Although most will agree with the absolute nature of this statement, if you watch your life's events and recall yourself having wronged someone, you may not remember how that person wronged you in return. That's actually quite normal. Nonetheless, the law still applies — every time. Here's the how and why, but let me add to the previous quote to complete its intended message and you'll see what I mean: *"As you do unto others, it will be done unto you — but not necessarily from the same persons."*

In observation of my own life, I have had to pay for every mistake I have ever made, every lapse of integrity and every moment of dishonesty, toward others or myself. But the universe's payback rarely came from those I wronged. Pay attention to this simple truism in your life, and eventually you will give yourself the proof that every word that is written here is true.

The ultimate benefit of this piece of wisdom is that it allows you to create your future in the way you want because the law also works in reverse. For everyone you help, for every time you display honesty and integrity, for every good deed you do — especially those no one else knows about — it will all come back to you eventually, and also not from the same people. This all has to do with the law of abundance, which we will discuss in the next chapter.

If you do the right thing now and avoid all that is out of integrity, you will secure a future of good things coming your way. What you put out is what you will eventually receive back. By taking responsibility for everything in your life and not going around with a victim mentality, you open yourself up to success, wealth, and a life of abundance.

Despite the controversy my words will inevitably generate in some minds, here is another way of looking at the separation of those who have the potential to succeed and those who don't. If your thought process is profoundly liberal, then you are on the wrong side. Hardly any successful entrepreneurs have a liberal mindset. For example, political correctness is one of the most profound evils that comes from the liberal camp that will keep you from succeeding. Political correctness essentially means talking and acting in a way that offends no one and demanding that other people talk and act in the same way so that you are not offended. How many hugely successful entrepreneurs have you heard being politically correct? Probably none.

Think about what a giant pile of BS that entire concept is. How is it possible to never be offended and never to offend someone else, even unintentionally? It is not. But there is a solution! The solution is to turn your thinking around 180 degrees. In other words, STOP BEING OFFENDED. Who cares what other people may think of you, your race, your status, your words, sexual orientation, language, religion, or anything else. If everyone just stopped getting offended, the problem would be solved overnight. It is an absolute impossibility that no one will ever offend anyone else again. The whole concept of political correctness was designed with a sinister motive and that is to create conflict between us. It was not created for the sake of harmony between us.

Stop caring what others think of you because if you believe in political correctness, you see yourself as a victim and therefore live with a welfare mentality. The world owes you something. Except that it doesn't. No one owes you anything. But you owe it to yourself to evolve beyond such limited thinking — if you want to become successful.

Back to our discussion on how most wealthy individuals are actually hardworking, honest, and contributing members of our society. For the few individuals among you who may think that the ultra-rich don't seem to fall into this category and you therefore feel that you've poked holes in my argument, I say you are right — but my argument still stands. Let me explain. My discussion does not include many of the ultra-rich, mega-millionaires or billionaires. They are dramatically different from the millionaire next door I am referring to.

Many billionaires are at the root of much of the evil facing our world today because of how dramatically different they are from the wealthy I am referring to. Many billionaires acquired their wealth through unfair competition, favors, government exemptions, and manipulation of our markets. The robber barons of a century ago are prime examples. Their offspring are some of the individuals I am referring to in today's world.

What makes billionaires so dramatically different is that their vast wealth has caused them to live a life that is completely removed from the reality you and I live in. They see themselves as having been anointed into their position so as to rule over us. Worse still is that many of them are sociopaths — they have no conscience and do not care who they step on and how many people they hurt on their quest for more wealth and power. In my opinion it is our conscience — our desire and ability to do the right thing — that is God's presence in man. Without conscience you can do the math as to who these people really are and whom they worship. Anyway, these are not the people I am talking about when I refer to the wealthy. But even among billionaires there are exceptions, such as Steve Jobs, Richard Branson, and Elon Musk, each of whom I admire tremendously.

The Law of Abundance

"Whatever we plant in our subconscious
mind and nourish with repetition
and emotion will one day become a reality."

–Earl Nightingale

This is a continuation of the issue of mind-set. Its importance cannot be stressed enough as your mind-set is a make-it-or-break-it issue. Without the right mind-set, success and wealth will remain a distant fantasy.

Also known as the law of attraction, the law of abundance is a universal law available to anyone who knows how to use it. It allows you to attract abundance into your life rather than you having to go out and chase it. We've all heard of the law, but most people have no idea how it works.

In essence, the law of abundance means that what we put out and what we believe is what we will receive. Our beliefs, in the form of thoughts and emotions, create a void that the universe will conspire to fill. It is a real law that has been proven to work countless times by countless people. You only need to learn how to properly apply it, and as usual, there's more to it than meets the eye.

Most people think that abundance and happiness come from our external environment, that we will be happy and fulfilled when we have what we want from our material world and when people treat us the way we want them to treat us. We are taught to believe that we live in an outside-in world. The outside world creates our internal environment —

our happiness or lack thereof — but the truth is the exact opposite. We live in an inside-out world. Our insides create the outside. Our internal environment — our thoughts and emotions — create our external reality. This includes the material goods we have in our lives, our level of wealth, and the quality of our relationships.

Attracting abundance depends on the internal environment you create. That environment is dominated by your thoughts, which will then transform into emotions. Those in turn transform your external reality to coincide with your thoughts and emotions.

It all starts with your thoughts. Numerous books have been written about this, and they are at the very foundation of the entire personal-development industry. Pick up *Think and Grow Rich; As a Man Thinketh; The Strangest Secret; As You Think So Shall You Become; The Secret;* or a plethora of others. They all talk about the same thing. Your thoughts create your external reality. Think dependency and you will be dependent. Think abundance and you will receive abundance. What matters most is how you think those thoughts. More on that in a minute.

We are like magnets. We attract what we put out. In fact, the revelation that your thoughts create your external reality should tell you that we were made to be co-creators. This is an extremely powerful realization as it gives us the knowledge that we can alter our future to create any outcome we desire. What we sow now, through our positive thoughts and emotions, creates what we reap later, in the form of love, happiness, material goods, wealth, friendships, and more. Likewise, if what we sow is negative, then the outcome will also be negative.

Here's how it all works: If you experience the emotion of having something in your life that is currently not there, then you will attract it to fill that void, just like a magnet. For example, if you cause yourself to feel the emotions of what it's like to be in love with your soul mate, this mobilizes the universe to bring your soul mate into your life.

Happiness does not happen when you get this or that. It's the other way around. You get whatever you think will bring you happiness by creating the emotion of happiness first. Think about how this or that would make you feel, and you will immediately start to attract it.

As mentioned, it all starts with your thoughts, but it is not just what you think that attracts what you are thinking about but also how you think it. This is important because your subconscious mind cannot differentiate between different ways of expressing the same thing. It just hears the words from your conscious mind and acts on them to manifest them into reality. For example, if it is health you want, don't think, "I don't want to be sick." Your mind hears the word "sick" and acts on it, moving you toward illness. Rather, think, "I want to be healthy," or better yet, think, "I am healthy," as if it were already a reality. Let your mind hear the word "healthy" and then it will act on that to manifest health into your life.

The same holds true with success and abundance. Don't think, "I don't want to be poor anymore" or "I don't want to live paycheck to paycheck" anymore. This only attracts poverty or a nine-to-five existence. Think positive words. Think, "I want to be successful. I am successful. I am wealthy." Imagine what it would be like to be successful and wealthy, and feel it as if you already had it.

I am guessing that this is also the foundation of the well-known mantra we've all heard from the French psychologist and pharmacist Emile Coue. He coined the phrase "Every day, in every way, I am getting better and better." It provides rapid results if said with regular repetition, conviction, and real emotion.

In essence, this is an exercise in autosuggestion. But there's more, and this next part should definitely not be ignored or neglected, as it is a key ingredient to making the law of abundance work for you.

One of the key aspects to creating abundance in your life is an expression of gratitude for all that you have, have had, and will have. You can do this in prayer or in any way you choose, but it should be done almost daily. Express gratitude for everything the universe has given you, including the lessons you have had to learn and even the mistakes, failures, setbacks, and hardships that gave you those lessons. Express gratitude for the beauty in the world and the amazing abilities of your mind. Be grateful for the universal laws I described to you and your ability to use them for your benefit.

The key to the power of gratitude is this: It has been said that the more things that you express gratitude for, the more you will have to express gratitude for. That is, one blessing you are thankful for begets more blessings to be thankful for. Just try it and see the amazing results.

You have been provided with a snapshot of the power of the law of abundance and how you can make it work for you. Obviously entire books can and have been written on this topic, so you may choose to study it further. I would recommend some of the books I mentioned in addition to doing some of your own online research. The more you know about the mechanics of the law of abundance, the more powerful the law becomes as a tool for manifesting the reality you desire.

Motivation and the
Power of Passion

"Follow your passion;
it will lead to your purpose."

–Oprah

This chapter contains the key points from an entire book I wrote on the subject of motivation and passion called *Motivation: Your Master Key to Success and Riches*. To my surprise, as I was writing the book I came up with several insights on the subject of passion and motivation that I had never seen in print before. I will share some of these with you here.

The book you are reading is all about living your passion and learning how to do so with virtually no chance of failure. The key to making success a predetermined reality is passion itself. When you do what you love, several things happen simultaneously to skyrocket your chances for success.

The first is that your passion will keep you from quitting. When you do what you love, you're doing it because you love it. You won't want to do anything else, and therefore you'll do whatever it takes to keep doing it. As obvious as that may sound, the profundity of this insight should not be underestimated because doing what you love, or the passion you feel for what you do, creates one of the strongest forces available to you that will always steer you in the right direction and keep you going no matter what. That force is motivation.

On the power of being motivated, Alexander Graham Bell said this: "What this power is I cannot say. All I know is that it exists and it becomes available only when a man is in that state of mind in which he knows exactly what he wants and is fully determined not to quit until he gets it."

Being properly motivated is the key to your success, wealth, and happiness. I learned this from my own entrepreneurial career and even took this to the extreme. For every business I have ever contemplated starting, I always had one overriding criteria that determined whether it was something I would get into — my interest in the business itself. It had to be something I was deeply interested in with the potential to turn into a genuine passion. Not knowing it at the time, this secured my success in every instance. For one, it provided me with the motivation to get up in the morning and go to work. In fact, I looked forward to going to work every day.

What set me apart from other entrepreneurs (and this is where I took things a bit to the extreme) was that it was always a business that I knew little to nothing about. I went into the mail-order and sweepstakes business with zero experience and turned it into a multimillion-dollar venture mailing over three million pieces of mail per month. I went into the charitable arena with no knowledge of that business, and within one year my company was supporting 2,100 needy kids around the world. I became a radio talk-show host from one day to the next and even traded precious metals and diamonds with immense success, all with no prior experience or knowledge whatsoever. If years ago someone had told me that I'd know how to accurately grade and price diamonds within a few years, I would have probably laughed, but it did happen. The same with the four books I wrote prior to this one. Each of them became a best seller on Amazon. Today I expect success in any venture I undertake because I live by the lessons in this book.

Whatever I chose to get into, it just always sounded amazingly interesting to me. Because I was interested in the business itself, it also allowed me to learn everything I needed to become an expert — *very quickly*. This is another important advantage that manifests when you follow your interests: you learn in no time. Have you ever read something you don't care about, and you end up rereading it over and over again, but the information still won't sink in? But if you read something you are interested in, then you can't get enough of it, and you remember every word. This provided me with a powerful advantage in my choice of businesses, and you can make it work for you also.

Furthermore, money was never a deciding factor for me. Obviously I made sure my new business could have good financial potential, but that was never why I entered a specific business. I quickly learned that when you do something you love and are passionate about, the money will automatically follow. I intuitively knew this all along as I had always witnessed rich people who were miserable because all they cared about was money, material possessions, and outdoing their friends and neighbors. But doing what you love provides more than just motivation; it provides fulfillment, and fulfillment is infinitely more valuable than money. It is a feeling deep in your soul that you are doing what you are meant to be doing, and you are loving every minute of it. The money is secondary at best.

In summary, doing what you love provides you with the motivation to get up every morning and to do what it takes to build a successful business. It gives you the ability to learn and become an expert in your field very quickly, as well as the means to keep from quitting just because you may run into an obstacle. The reward is fulfillment, which is my definition of success, and that is doing what you love and making a good living doing it. Chances are you'll probably even get rich doing it.

So why is it that so few people know how to get and stay properly motivated so that they can accomplish anything they want in life? Honestly, the right level of motivation is sometimes all we need to make our dreams come true. But how many of us actually do that? Obviously very few.

The answer to why so few of us are properly motivated, once again, is lack of knowledge. We will therefore delve into an analysis of motivation at a level that only a few people know about. It is an understanding of where motivation comes from so that we can tap into it, and it also involves knowing about the different types of motivation. This knowledge will empower anyone to live their purpose and their passion and to fulfill their dreams. It truly is your master key to success and riches.

Most of us live a life where most of the motivation we experience is negative, such as the threat of getting fired from our job. We adjust our behavior to avoid a negative outcome. This is the lowest form of motivation and never accomplishes much except to avoid what we don't want. In the end, all we achieve the maintenance of the status quo. But it doesn't move us forward.

Only in marketing and advertising is there a valuable need for showing a potential audience how to avoid a negative outcome. Consider an advertisement for a nutritional supplement that might keep us from getting a specific ailment. We are thankful for the knowledge, and there is nothing wrong with this advertising approach as it can definitely help us. But we shouldn't live our lives with negative motivation.

The real power to achieve and accomplish comes from positive motivation, of which there are three kinds. Each of them, properly understood and applied, can accomplish miracles, but they also have different levels of power. We will discuss them from least to greatest; the greatest being a source of motivation that is so powerful that it can make an individual unstoppable.

External Motivation – The first source of motivation, one we are all familiar with, is external motivation. This means that the motivating force comes from outside us. It can come from self-help books, audio recordings we might listen to in our cars, a coach, and even motivational seminars. Essentially we hear motivational information designed to mobilize us into action based on the positive outcome we are promised if we follow the outlined path. A great example is a motivational seminar conducted by a self-help guru such as Tony Robbins. Thousands of individuals can be simultaneously inspired, motivated, and pumped up with so much energy that they cannot contain their excitement. However, there's a big problem with external motivation, such as from seminars, which no one tells you about.

Have you ever seen someone come back from a motivational seminar, such as a Tony Robbins event? They come back inspired, motivated, excited, and full of energy. They have been given all the tools they need to turn their life around and become a fountain of achievement. They will tell you about the wonders of what they learned and let you know all the great things they're going to do. They are armed with all the right information and are pumped up to such a degree that they look like they're going to jump out of their skin.

They really did get all the right information — except for one key piece of knowledge that no one ever tells you — which is why a few weeks later their life is back to where it was before the seminar. The motivation has worn off, and virtually no changes have been made to the trajectory of their lives. Everything goes back to their previous status quo.

This sad outcome happens to almost everyone who goes to motivational seminars, and for this reason it can almost be said that seminars don't work. In fact, you could make a case for all motivational information, including books and audio materials, creating a peak of excitement but then landing you right back to where you started. Why? What happened? The information is typically spot-on, awesome, inspiring, motivating, energizing, and full of ideas and plans that theoretically can take anyone from mediocrity to the stars. Then why doesn't it happen most of the time? The reason is as I told you: one critical piece of information is missing. Why they don't give you this information is a mystery to me, but nonetheless here it is. With this single piece of missing information virtually ALL motivational material can change your life in ways most only dream about.

What they don't tell you is that external motivation — motivation that comes from an outside source, such as a seminar — is like food and water. You can't just eat and drink once and expect not to need to repeat it the next day. Likewise, you cannot go to the gym for a week and expect the gains to last. You have to continue exercising. In the same fashion you have to continue exercising your brain with ongoing input of motivational information. It has to be a regular process for it to have a lasting effect. You need to absorb motivational or self-help materials almost every day for the effects to last. The motivational information can come from books, audio materials, coaches, or occasional seminars. It doesn't really matter much where you get it as long as it becomes an ongoing process. In fact, it should become a lifelong process.

The information we are discussing, such as from the hundreds of self-help courses available, is almost always near perfect, complete, and amazingly effective — but only if you continue consuming it on a daily basis. It is beyond me why self-help gurus don't mention this simple truism, but now that you know it, make sure you never ignore this vitally important lesson.

Internalized Motivation – The second type of motivation, more powerful than the first, is one that starts out external but then becomes internal — it comes from the outside but becomes part of our being when internalized. The outside portion is something we are interested in. It becomes internal when this interest expands into a true passion. Once it is a passion, it becomes part of our being and stays inside us. Passions do not fade away like external motivation, which needs to be repeated constantly. Passion becomes a part of who we are.

We have already discussed the power of passion. It is something we can all develop. If we are not already deeply passionate about something, we can start with something we are very interested in and then internalize that interest so that it becomes a true passion. Then the full force of the power of passion is unleashed in the form of a motivational force that makes you nearly unstoppable. This keeps you from quitting and gets you up in the morning because you look forward to working on your passion; it also allows you to learn all you need to learn very quickly. Being passionate about something is where it's at if you want to become successful. That should be amply clear by now.

Internal Motivation – The most powerful form of motivation is one that has always been inside us, even if we don't recognize it yet. This is what genuinely makes an individual unstoppable. Its power is one of the greatest forces in the universe as it permeates every fiber of our being — and always has. It just needs to be recognized and unleashed. In a bit I will help you recognize your already existing internal motivation that is currently present in the form of core values and core desires.

A core desire is like an obsession, one we cannot let go of even if we tried. We refuse to let anything stand in our way, not even procrastination or rationalization, two of the greatest deterrents to becoming successful.

Once we recognize our core values and core desires, we have to follow them. Failing to follow them would lead us into the depth of depression. An example is one's desire to have children. If you can only see yourself with children, then you will have children one day no matter what. For this reason you could never marry someone who doesn't want children. The marriage simply wouldn't last. Core values and desires are so strong that they are forces we have no choice but to follow because they are the forces that give our lives meaning. They define who we are.

Personal-growth author, speaker, and coach Jack Zufelt calls this the conquering force. When you follow your core desires, you are not pushing yourself — you are being called to do something. It is an alignment with your purpose that never extinguishes. Action becomes effortless. According to Zufelt, as you approach 100 percent desire, the force exerted increases exponentially like a Richter scale. The difference between a 75 percent and a 100 percent level of desire is a factor of 1,000. Your desires are your fuel. The higher your level of desire, the more fuel you have.

Most people do not fully realize what their core desires are although glimpses will inevitably show throughout their lives. There are a few exercises you can do to help you discover this ultimate motivational fountain. Since your core desires contain the greatest force available to you that can make your success an absolute predetermined certainty, it makes sense to discover what they are and to make sure that they are at least an ingredient in whatever it is you will do.

To discover what truly motivates us we have to dig pretty deep. Fortunately, the exercises are pretty simple. Start by asking yourself, "Who am I?" and write down the first words that come to mind. When I was given this exercise at a seminar many years ago, the word "teacher" came to mind and later the word "creator." I am, by definition, a teacher and a creator. Considering that writing this book is an act of creation and I am using it to teach you lessons on how to become successful, I have thus incorporated my two core desires into the activity of writing a book and imparting my knowledge to you.

Next, ask yourself, "If money were not an object, what would I be doing?" Whatever comes to mind, even if it doesn't sound like a business, write it down. Anything can be incorporated into a business. For example, if the word "travel" comes to mind, there are endless possibilities that incorporate travel into a business, such as opening a travel agency, being a tour guide, or becoming a travel writer. Any passion can be an ingredient in a business, so don't hold back.

Another exercise is to give some thought to what you'd like your eulogy to be. What would you like people to remember about you? In a perfect world, what would you like to have been your life's accomplishments?

A critical aspect to these exercises is to always ask yourself, "Why?" If travel was your answer, ask yourself why you chose travel as something you'd like to do because your answer may not be your final core desire but merely a stepping-stone. For example, if I asked you what you'd most like to accomplish and you said you want to become a successful investor, I'd immediately ask you why. Your answer might be because you want to get rich. I would again ask you why you want to get rich. Your immediate response might be so that you can spend all your time with your family — and that would have brought us to your true core desire. Becoming an investor was a mere stepping-stone to becoming rich, which in turn was a stepping-stone to making all your time available so that you can spend it with the family — your real core desire.

The exercises I just outlined for you are discussed in more detail in my book on motivation. If you want to dig deeper into discovering your core desires, then definitely check it out. It's a quick read, but it's filled with useful information. It will also detail the reasons why money should not and simply cannot be your primary motivating force. Furthermore, if you want to delve even deeper into the subject of passion and core desires, check out Jack Zufelt's material on the conquering force.

Hopefully you will have realized by now how important it is to act on your passions and find your core motivating forces. This area deserves a lot of attention, and I strongly urge you not to set it aside without first achieving complete mastery so that you discover what truly drives you. The effort is worth it a million times over. Don't let neglect turn into regret.

"Let the beauty of what you love be what you do."

–Rumi

Teamwork Makes
the Dream Work

A few years ago there was a great medical TV drama series called *House*. In it lead physician Gregory House, played by Hugh Laurie, was known as one of the best problem solvers in the medical industry and definitely the best in the hospital where he worked, but he didn't always come up with the solution to his patient's medical dilemma all by himself. He had a team of three physicians who worked for him. He consulted with them for their ideas and diagnoses. They didn't often come up with the correct final diagnosis, but that is not why he hired them or why he used them. Whenever they had brainstorming sessions, it was often something they said, even if it was unrelated or way off base, that sparked an idea in House, which ultimately led to the correct diagnosis for their patient.

I have always used a similar method to solve problems or come up with new ideas. I listen to what other people have to say, never expecting that their idea will be the answer I seek. I use them because their words frequently create a connection or spark a groundbreaking idea or solution in my own mind. I guess it is a talent I have developed that I believe anyone can develop for their own benefit with just a little bit of practice. It is the essence of group brainstorming.

Brainstorming sessions, properly conducted, involve a group of people who get together and each of them submits their idea or solution to whatever is being discussed. The correct way of doing it is to encourage everyone to say whatever comes to mind — even if it may seem obviously wrong, trivial, or even ridiculous — because of the aforementioned mental connections that may get created. Anything can spark a good idea, even a totally unrelated thought.

Furthermore, a good entrepreneur will recognize when another person does have a good idea. That alone is a talent worth cultivating. Entrepreneurs are not always lone wolves with the talent to repeatedly invent something or solve every problem. Often they just have a knack for recognizing the right solution or idea when someone else mentions it. A good entrepreneur uses this technique regularly because they don't let their egos get in the way. That is, they don't suffer from a "not invented here syndrome." It doesn't matter to them where the idea comes from as long as it's good. Obviously, they will also give credit wherever credit is due.

I do this a lot. I not only listen to other people when I'm trying to solve a problem or come up with a new idea, but I also pay attention to everything around me, even while I drive. Anything — something you hear or something you see — can be the spark that moves you forward. I have even had song lyrics spark an idea and even the topic for chapters in some of my books.

Here's another aspect to consider when it comes to having a team to brainstorm with or even having partners in business. In my past as a serial entrepreneur, I have always operated alone. I liked the idea of knowing that if something needed to get done, I would always step up to the plate and do it. You don't always get that certainty when you have to rely on others. My determination, resilience, and love of work for its own sake have enabled me to chalk up repeated successes. But there is a downside to going at it alone.

You've undoubtedly heard the saying that it's lonely at the top. There is definitely truth to that as you can only get so close to your employees. In the end you're their boss, and a certain separation is required to maintain the integrity of that hierarchy.

In my last business, things were different. A couple friends of mine had always wanted to go into business with me because they recognized my expertise. In turn, I was very attracted to the idea of being able to share everything with someone else. In fact, it should come as no surprise that the joys of success are that much greater when they are shared. Having partners also allows you to have a built-in brainstorming team to get past challenges.

In the end, bringing on two partners was the right decision. The company was able to grow way beyond what I would have done myself, and the whole thing was that much more fun. I enjoyed getting up every single day to go to work. One critical element was how I structured the partnership: It guaranteed that there would be no impasses when an occasional disagreement arose. I describe this structure in detail in my first *20/20 Hindsight* book and will reproduce this information in the next chapter. Its importance cannot be overstated, so it deserves its own chapter.

The concept of a team as described (brainstorming groups or partners) can be tremendously useful if properly structured, but it is not mandatory to succeed. I have succeeded numerous times without any help whatsoever — with one exception, and that was having a mentor. I doubt I could have reached the heights that I did without a mentor, even if some of my mentors never knew that I was watching and learning from them.

Having a mentor is mandatory because it is how you learn. I elaborated on this in the introduction: you must learn from those who have done it already, preferably with multiple successes and even a few failures. This book can even be viewed as mentorship as I am imparting lessons I learned from both successes and failures. But a real live mentor, unlike a book, is interactive and therefore even more valuable. You can ask questions and get advice.

Finding a mentor is not difficult. Almost every successful entrepreneur wants to give back in return for the blessings they have received and are more than willing to help others succeed. You only have to ask. Trust me — you'll be surprised by how willing most successful people are to help you on your journey. But choose wisely. Pick someone with integrity who has only one motive — to help others join the ranks of the successful and wealthy. There is great joy in imparting one's wisdom to others and seeing the fruits of your guidance turn into a blossoming success story. That is why we do it.

Alternatively, you can do what I sometimes did. I had some individuals in my life, such as a vendor, whom I never asked to mentor me. I simply watched them like a hawk and asked them questions whenever we got together. Maybe they knew; maybe they didn't. Nonetheless, the amount I learned from them was phenomenal.

Teamwork makes the dream work. It has been said that you are the product of what you read and the people you surround yourself with. The right people in your social circle will pull you up, whereas the wrong people will drag you down. This doesn't mean that you cannot go it alone, as I have done numerous times, but know that you cannot become successful all on your own. You always need others to support your business. There are mentors you must learn from, employees who must support your vision, vendors who must be there for you when you need them, and obviously customers who must buy your product or service. In a sense, they are all part of your team, directly or indirectly, and their connection to you can be a vital ingredient to your venture.

There is one group of entrepreneurs where having more people to associate with is more important. That group is females. Men often view solitude as a joy, but women are innately more social than men. For this reason, entrepreneurship in its purest "lone wolf" form is often more of a struggle for women. They can easily feel isolated. I understand that this is a generalization and doesn't apply to all females, but probably to the majority.

Females that fall into this category should therefore consider having a partner or making sure they regularly associate with social support groups, such as entrepreneurial clubs, chambers of commerce, etc. Ideally, they should have others in their inner circle that are of equal status, unlike employees, so they can discuss anything with them without having to maintain a certain professional separation. I am mentioning this for the benefit of my female readers who fall into this category so they don't put themselves into a disadvantageous position when considering their potential for happiness in the entrepreneurial world. Entrepreneurs don't have to be isolated if they don't want to be, and some females should plan for this from the start. It may be lonely at the top for some people, but it doesn't have to be.

Finally, let's discuss the value of a team when it comes to finding investors. Some new businesses need capital, which the entrepreneur may not have. In that case you will need a business plan to help attract that capital, which we will talk about in more detail later. Right now what matters is the value that your team's skills, history, past successes, etc. bring to the table to help bring your idea its needed investors. Your team and their qualifications should be highlighted prominently in your business plan. Most people think it is the quality of the idea that matters above all else. It is not. Allow me to tell you a little story I made up and love to repeat because of the profound point it makes.

Imagine you did not know me (or anything about me) and I approach you somewhere and we chat. After a few minutes I tell you about a business idea I have. It turns out that it is nothing short of brilliant and could create endless fortunes for all involved. I ask you to invest $20,000 in my idea, which you acknowledge is the best business idea you've ever heard.

Would you invest? Probably not. In fact, the vast majority of people would not invest in my idea for a simple reason: they don't know me. You probably would not either for the same reason. You don't know my history of successes or failures, my character, my integrity, my motives, or anything else about me. Despite the quality of my idea, the risk is too high when investing in a complete stranger.

Now imagine Bill Gates approaches you on the street. He tells you that he has a new business idea, but he's not going to tell you what it is. You have no idea whether his idea is good or bad. He says nothing else except to ask you if you want to invest $20,000. Would you? Of course you would. It's Bill Gates! You might even ask him if you can invest more than just $20,000.

The lesson is clear. People invest in people, not in ideas. Ideas are actually a dime a dozen. We've all had great ideas.

It's the people who know how to turn them into reality that are priceless. It is the same with a business plan. Every business plan has a detailed explanation of the concept with a feasibility study, market research, and financial projections. It also contains team members' bios. Which is more important, the idea or the executive team? It is the team, by an overwhelming majority.

If your team includes people with a series of successes in their backgrounds, successful people who are known to the reader of the plan, or people whose names lend immediate credibility to your plan, then finding capital is almost assured, *even if the idea is less than stellar.* You are more likely to attract what you need with a great team than with a great idea. This is very, very important. Many mediocre ideas have attracted millions in start-up capital because of the team. A great team can turn almost any idea into a fortune, but a lousy team cannot make a dime with even the best of ideas.

The reason that teamwork is included in this text as an absolute requirement is the aforementioned understanding that no one can become successful alone. Even if your multimillion-dollar company is a one-man show, you still did not get there by yourself. Again, you have to have customers who purchase your product. You need vendors who agree to do business with you. You must have people you can learn from. And in most cases you need employees who support your vision and work for the benefit of your company. You have to learn to deal with all of these people in a respectful, honest manner so that they agree to do business with you without sabotaging you and your dream. Understanding this lesson will empower you to create the kind of team that will help turn your dream into reality.

*"Teamwork makes the dream work, but
a vision becomes a nightmare
when the leader has a big dream and a bad team."*

–John C. Maxwell

Partnerships Don't Work …
Unless You Do This!

This chapter on partnerships is a near identical reproduction from my book **20/20 Hindsight***. This is not something I would normally do, but I am duplicating most of the original here because of its importance. If you enter into a partnership and you don't know this information, you will likely fail. For this reason, it is one of those "must learn" lessons because the alternative is not just a temporary setback but the total collapse of your dream. Also, this is the lesson that inspired me to write and publish books on entrepreneurship in the first place, so I am honoring the lesson that got my writing career started by presenting it to you largely unaltered.*

Partnerships frequently fail because of the way most people go about them. In fact, the majority of partnerships are dead on arrival. So let's examine why many partnerships fail and what needs to be done from the beginning to protect them.

The rationale for having a partner makes all the sense in the world. What better way to go into business than by sharing risks and expenses while having your partner contribute additional time and expertise to the venture? In theory that sounds great, but reality is not so kind.

Partnerships are a virtually guaranteed recipe for disaster within as little as a few short months because of the most unexpected and unlikely of reasons. Almost every would-be entrepreneur who has tried going into business with someone else has failed at it and wondered what happened while blaming it all on the other partner.

The truth is that partnerships fail because of the most surprising of foundations, good intentions. In fact, it's precisely what you believed to be your partnership's strength that ends up being its Achilles' heel. Good intentions end up replacing good business sense. Ironically it was Karl Marx who said that the road to hell is paved with good intentions, and he was right. Welcome to business hell!

Consider the typical scenario of going into business with a partner. You choose someone you deem similarly qualified as you, someone whom you know, like, and trust. You want to motivate them to work as hard as you, so you go into an equal partnership where everything gets shared equally: decisions, labor, risks, and rewards. You want your partner to feel that they are your equal, so there will be no boss at the partnership level. Equality rules, and you both share and show nothing but the sincerest good intentions. You feel that both your business futures and your friendship are secure because you know that neither of you has the authority to exert their will over the other person. What can possibly go wrong?

Precious few people have figured out why this formula is a recipe for business and personal disaster, and even fewer have managed to avoid its pitfalls the first time they enter into a partnership.

Years ago I started a small computer sales and service company with a friend. We sold PCs to individuals and small businesses and provided networking, education, and configuration services. My friend and partner was the computer expert, and I had more general business experience than he. This appeared to be a good combination and provided us with a clear division of labor. He had the technical mind, and I had the business mind. And we both had nothing but good intentions.

Our business barely lasted three months. We even ended up in court together. Our problems began over the silliest issue, the design of our logo. We decided that I would design it, but when I did, my partner didn't like it. In fact, he didn't hesitate to claim that he could do better. Obviously I had an issue with this because I actually had some real-life creative design experience. He did not. That's why I was assigned with the task in the first place. I knew what I was doing, and once completed, I was emotionally attached to my design.

Our disagreement eventually turned into hostility as our egos went to war. What we surely both agreed should have been an insignificant disagreement eventually spiraled out of control. This minor dispute literally killed the company.

So here are the ingredients that are at the root of failed partnerships: good intentions, human nature, and ego. The offer of equality comes from our good intentions to make the partnership work. Unfortunately, a partnership where everything is shared equally rarely works, but it's precisely these types of partnerships that everyone starts.

Consider that what eventually happens in an equal partnership is a pure expression of human nature. We all have an ego — part of it strong, part of it weak or fragile. A strong ego is a healthy ego. It's an expression of self-confidence. A fragile ego is at the root of self-indulgence where self-righteousness and a "know it all" and "I'm always right" attitude surfaces.

Fragile egos cause business breakups, relationship breakups, and even wars between nations.

We all have strong and fragile egos in different proportions. Whatever those proportions are, some part, no matter how small, is on the fragile side. This is the side of us that gets emotionally attached, offended, defensive, and self-righteous. Some live their entire lives in this state of egoism. We all eventually demonstrate the darker side of our humanity, even if some of us do so only to a small degree. But this is the part of us that makes an equal partnership a mathematical impossibility to operate as intended.

What typically happens is that two people determine that they would be great partners in a new business for any number of reasons. They get along great, never argue, and complement each other on experience and expertise. Neither partner, because of their good intentions, would dare suggest anything but equality. A simple partnership agreement may even be drawn up outlining how everything will be shared equally. The overriding focus in that agreement will be equality in decision-making and equality in reaping the financial rewards. But it's precisely because of the well-crafted and well-intentioned equality clauses that the partnership will sink into oblivion.

The path toward destruction typically follows a common pattern. The business is started and everything is shared as equally as possible, especially decisions. The beginning of the partnership actually does work temporarily while many major decisions have to be made. The euphoria of having started a new business together makes disagreements almost unthinkable. Each partner respectfully involves the other person, and agreement on the major issues is overwhelmingly frequent.

Once the major decisions have been made, the time comes for some minor decisions, such as the design of a logo. Suddenly a disagreement pops up, and both sides will readily demonstrate emotional attachment to their viewpoint. This is ego, and it's human nature. The problem is that there's no tiebreaker. Who should give in? Who wins the disagreement? There's no third party to cast a deciding vote, and neither of the two partners have veto power. Sooner or later, one or more fragile egos are unveiled. The underlying issue soon becomes secondary as a minor disagreement turns into a major battle of egos. Even if the partnership remains operational for a while, overcoming several of these petty issues will sooner or later end with unfortunate results.

Business partnerships typically do not have the intimate emotional bonds that relationships have to fall back on. In fact, when money is at stake, the situation can become rapidly unstable because we want to protect our personal investment.

Equal partnerships are made worse when friends or family are involved. As they say, "The best thing about doing business with someone who knows you is that they know you. And the worst thing about doing business with someone who knows you is that they know you."

There are a couple ways to make a partnership work, but few will heed this advice until they have failed at least once and gained the wisdom of 20/20 hindsight. The most effective way is to create a partnership with multiple departments where each department has a leader. This means that no area of the business should be without a boss who has final authority.

Let's say there are two partners in a business that involves marketing, advertising, accounting, sales, and technical knowhow. Each discipline should be viewed as its own department, and each department needs a boss. Responsibilities should be roughly equal on both sides. Partner A may have the final say in the areas of advertising, marketing, and sales. Partner B may have the final say in accounting, finance, and the technical side of the business. This needs to be put in writing. Each partner should have undisputed veto power in each of their respective departments or areas of greater expertise as agreed upon at the beginning … and clearly spelled out in a partnership agreement.

There's still plenty of room for good intentions and mutual respect. It can be agreed and practiced that all decisions will still be made with the involvement of the other partner. However, if there's an irreconcilable disagreement, then the partner with veto power in that particular field gets no resistance from the other side when enforcing his will. In that department he is boss. Now the partnership has a chance of working.

As mentioned previously, partnerships with friends and family are particularly fragile and hard to make work. Sadly, more often than not, the friendship is destroyed along with the company. That's why any kind of business deals — not just partnerships — that involve friends and family must be put into writing. They have to be treated in the same way as a business venture with someone who is a complete stranger to you. Only then is the friendship protected. Here is an example.

My best friend is Jim. Several years ago he married his fiancée Denise, and I was best man at their wedding. Unfortunately, Jim wasn't doing great financially at the time, and for some reasons beyond Jim's control, his credit was also less than stellar. Of course, Jim and Denise wanted what all newlyweds want, a home to call their own. I gently introduced a seed into our conversation, the possibility of me financing a home for them. I thought of a way to make it a win-win scenario, which incidentally is the only type of agreements that I make. My philosophy is that nobody should ever walk away feeling that he or she got the better end of the deal. I believe in karma, and therefore if you take advantage of someone, it will eventually come back to bite you.

Anyway, my idea was to buy my friends a home that they would rent from me for one year and then purchase from me at slightly less than fair market appreciation. One side saved a little while the other side made a little, win-win. Additionally, my friends had the opportunity for home ownership without actually being able to qualify for it at that time. And they would have a year's worth of rent payments essentially going toward equity. If, at the end of the first year, they weren't yet in a position to buy the home from me, they agreed to rent for an additional year with the right to purchase the home at any time on the same terms during that second year. If after the second year they still couldn't or didn't want to buy the home, my friends could walk away from it, and I'd be able to sell the home on the open market. We fine-tuned the concept, and it all appeared to make sense. It was a go. And then we put it all in writing with every detail spelled out.

The end result was that my friends became happy homeowners for several years as they managed to buy the property from me after about a year and a half of rental occupancy. I made a modest profit on my investment, the down payment, and I was able to help my friends begin their new life together as homeowners. It worked out better than expected as the property appreciated beyond all our expectations, so Jim and Denise's equity position continued to grow. Throughout this transaction nothing was assumed, nothing was agreed upon without putting it in writing, and a win-win situation was thereby not left to chance or good intentions. Jim and I are still the best of friends.

In case you're one of those rare individuals who has a partnership that appears to be working or even thriving, consider yourself very fortunate. You're in the minority. As with anything there are exceptions.

Don't create partnerships based only on good intentions. Create win-win partnerships that have a chance of surviving. Business is business, even with friends and family. Put it in writing, and above all, make sure every aspect of the business has one of the partners with final authority when inevitable disagreements arise.

In my most recent business venture I had two partners. Our structure was a little different from the structure I just described. This structure requires a certain amount of maturity that comes only from years of experience, so it's not for everyone. Nonetheless, I'll describe it here because there are several similarities.

In our three-way partnership, without a doubt I had by far the most business experience. The business concept was my idea, and I would have pursued it with or without partners. I invited two friends to join me, and Jim was one of them. Because I knew that my business experience was vital to the success of the partnership and the business in general, I insisted that I have veto rights over all major decisions. My partners wisely agreed because they knew my track record.

But here's what has made our partnership thrive beyond expectations over more than five years: In all those years I've used my veto power in only two or three instances. We still made all decisions together, and we eventually found common ground even if sometimes I didn't entirely agree. We still had our separate departments or areas of responsibility based on our areas of expertise. The only time I exercised my veto right was when I absolutely knew that my viewpoint was the correct way to go based on my many years in business.

I no longer need to be right every time. In fact, I know I'm not right every time, and I'm okay with that. I guess that's the difference between a strong and a fragile ego. Over the years my ego has evolved and become substantially stronger than it used to be. Remember, the fragile ego is at the root of partnership problems. A strong ego is the cement that can make a partnership thrive for many, many years.

You may ask yourself whether it's wise to go into a partnership in the first place, even if it's structured properly. Quite simply, the disadvantage of a partnership is that you'll share everything, including profits. The advantage of a partnership is the same: you'll share everything, the good and the bad. In the end I would advise you to consider this. A partnership provides leverage to go places that are often out of reach when you are running the show alone, and I'm referring mostly to the size of your company. You can build quicker with partners for several reasons. My last business was a gold-buying business, and at its peak we had fifty retail locations, something I would probably not have strived for had I been without partners.

Here is another vital partnership lesson: Aside from having additional hands in the fire to do the work, I think there's a more compelling reason to have one or more partners. It's not just that we all have different areas of expertise; more importantly, we all have different likes and dislikes. There's always some area within your business where you may not like to work. For some people it may be finances and accounting; for others it may be whatever manual labor is involved. It may also be something like sitting in government offices for hours every time you need a new license.

In my last business the division of labor went along the lines of expertise, but it also took likes and dislikes into consideration. The issue of expertise is obvious, but the issue of likes may not be. The point is this: If there's something you don't like doing, then that area will almost certainly hold back your growth potential because you'll avoid it at all cost. But for your partner it may be the opposite. It may be the exact area where they like working, and they'll never procrastinate doing what's needed in that area. This is very important to take into consideration. You can often go much farther with partners than without them. But you have to do it right. Make sure every department has someone leading it with final authority in case of disagreement, and make sure that every partner's area of expertise and the activities that they enjoy doing correspond with the departments they are in charge of. Follow these simple ingredients and give your partnership a genuine chance to thrive.

The Secret to Solving
Any Problem

"Problems are only opportunities in work clothes."

–Henri Kaiser

As an entrepreneur, you will always be confronted with problems that need to be solved, questions that need to be answered, and hurdles that need to be overcome. Even as non-entrepreneurs, we all have to come up with answers and solutions throughout our lives.

You should start the journey described in this chapter with the knowledge that every problem has a solution, every question has an answer, and just about every obstacle can be overcome. And yes, you have it within you to come up with whatever solution is required for those hurdles. Additionally, if you know the right techniques, then any goal can be achieved, regardless of how ambitious that goal may be. The methodology to achieving your goals is quite similar to problem-solving as you'll see shortly. Whatever you can imagine, you can turn into reality. You may not have all the required mental tools available to you right now, but once you learn the necessary lessons, you will be unstoppable.

I will show you one of the most powerful problem-solving tools known to man — and amazingly it is not difficult to implement. In fact, once I describe it, you will recognize that you have probably used this technique many times before. I will show you how to consciously use it so that you can guide its awesome power toward whatever problem you need to resolve. Until now you have probably used this method without knowing that you were using it and most certainly without knowing why and how it works so well. We will also fine-tune the methodology to make this technique as effective as possible.

Once you harness this problem-solving tool, you will have the comfort of knowing that no matter what question needs an answer or no matter what problem needs a solution, you can overcome those challenges — every time! This, like the lesson on persistence and determination, should give you the comfort of knowing that nothing can stand in your way on your road toward success.

Let me start by describing how you have probably used this tool before, probably on multiple occasions. Consider this scenario: Have you ever forgotten someone's name and then tried as hard as you could to remember it until you just gave up? And then the weirdest thing happens: If you didn't come up with the name and you eventually just gave up trying to recall it, you then probably forgot about the issue — until you woke up in the middle of the night with the name appearing in your mind from out of nowhere. Wow, where did that come from?

The reality is that you used a most powerful tool available to everyone without knowing the what and how of it. That tool is your subconscious mind. The process of consciously trying to remember and then letting go actually mobilized your unconscious mind to solve the question for you without you knowing what you were doing.

Our mind consists or our conscious mind and our unconscious (or subconscious) mind. We are most aware of our conscious process of thought but hardly aware of the subconscious, yet the subconscious portion of our mind is 90 percent of the whole, making it infinitely more powerful than the conscious portion. It is like an iceberg. We see only the 10 percent that floats above the water but not the 90 percent — the vast majority — that is submerged below the surface. It is the same with our conscious and subconscious portions of our minds.

So here's what actually happened that made your subconscious remember the name you had forgotten. While you were banging your head against the wall trying to remember the forgotten name, you were actually sending a message to your subconscious mind to mobilize into action and resolve the problem for you. It did this in the background without you even knowing about it. When it did and you suddenly remembered the forgotten name in the middle of the night, it seemed to appear from out of nowhere. But the entire process was actually a well-orchestrated method that you can use to solve virtually any problem.

Let's say that as an entrepreneur you are suddenly faced with a problem, question, or hurdle that requires resolution. What you should do is consciously focus on the issue and try to come up with the answer. Think about it with as much focus and intensity as possible, almost to the point of exhaustion. If you come up with the answer — great — but typically you will need the power of your subconscious mind to come to the rescue.

Once you feel like the answer just won't present itself, mentally tell your subconscious mind to take over and then forget about the problem. Seriously, forget about it, but know that your subconscious will not. It will continue working in the background with much more power than your conscious trying could ever muster.

It is important that you really do let go of the problem and stop thinking about it. Only then will you unleash the full potential of your subconscious abilities. Sometime over the next day or so, the solution will pop into your mind, seemingly from out of nowhere. There you go — it's that simple, yet so powerful.

An important aspect of this technique is your belief in its effectiveness. As you have heard before, whatever the mind can conceive *and believe*, the mind can achieve. It is another absolute law you should learn to use to your advantage.

Entrepreneurs have learned to harness the power of their subconscious mind. They use it to solve problems and to invent ideas, methods, and products. In similar fashion they use the power of their subconscious to fulfill any goal. It is their fountain of creativity and achievement. It can be yours too.

> *"The problem is not that there are problems.*
> *The problem is expecting otherwise and thinking*
> *that having problems is a problem."*
> –Theodore Rubin

Dreams with Deadlines

*"Those who do not have goals are doomed
forever to work for those who do."*

–Brian Tracy

You cannot cover the topic of success without addressing the critical issue of goal setting. According to countless studies, of all the things that successful people have in common, goal setting and to-do lists always rank on top.

The best definition of a goal I know is that a goal is a dream with a deadline. Without deadlines all you have are dreams that will probably remain unfulfilled forever. Your deadline will push you to accomplish your dream within an achievable time frame. Deadlines should be set for interim steps and milestones as well as the final outcome.

Nothing happens without clear goals because if you don't know where you are going, how are you going to get there? A goal puts your destination in focus. That vision becomes the motivating force for you to consciously and subconsciously continue to move closer toward your goal day by day.

People with goals become leaders. To be a leader you must have goals. Those goals must be in the form of a crystal-clear vision of where you want your company to go, and that clarity will determine how well you lead your people. Leaders with a loyal and passionate following have developed this following because of their vision and their ability to communicate it. This includes employees. Consider the values and purpose that you and your company stand for. What is your mission? Make sure that everyone around you knows and understands where you are headed. Only in this way will they follow and support your goals.

You also need to have a plan that details how you're going to reach your goals. Having a plan and following it is the essence of making your goals come true. Again, deadlines are critical to making sure you don't stray or procrastinate.

I will not spend a lot of time on the details of how to achieve your goals as this chapter is more about the importance of setting goals rather than the methodology. I describe two methods in great detail in my first *20/20 Hindsight* book. In fact, these are by far the most effective methods I know, and they have worked countless miracles for me in my life. Outside of my favorite methods, there are numerous books out there you can also refer to for effective techniques. Nonetheless, I will go over some basic points regarding the two ways of accomplishing practically any goal I set my mind to that I have used for many years.

The first is quite simple and somewhat obvious. You break your goal down into some major steps, each with its own deadline, and then you break down those major steps into smaller steps. The smallest steps should be small enough to be easily achievable by any standard, which is why I call this the baby-step method. Mark Twain said, "The secret of getting ahead is getting started. The secret of getting started is breaking your complex overwhelming tasks into manageable tasks, and then starting on the first one."

This quote tells us a lot. First, as I mentioned, break your large steps or goals into smaller, manageable steps. Then, none of this will matter unless you take that first step. Every journey starts with that first step. Don't hold back; don't procrastinate; just do it. Take the first step, and the second one will come easily. The first step makes or breaks most people because they always find an excuse as to why they think they are not ready.

Vincent van Gogh said, with similar intent, "Great things are done by a series of small things brought together." Break down your major goal into small steps, and take one step at a time. It's like walking up the stairs. Put one foot in front of the other, and eventually you'll end up at the top. There is no other possible outcome if your goals have been broken down into small enough steps.

Finally, put your steps in writing. Put your goal at the top of your sheet of paper, then break it down into the major steps and add a deadline to each. Then break those major steps down into smaller, achievable steps. It should look almost like a to-do list of small steps underneath each of your major steps. Then move from bottom to top within each category. This list will become your road map and your plan.

The other method I use is a little more complicated but also vastly more powerful. Where the first baby-step method involves seeing the path you have to take and breaking it down into small steps, the second method is for goals where you don't see a clear path from A to B. It can even be used for goals that seem unachievable or out of reach. Sadly, these are the goals most often abandoned by the general public because they just don't know how to make them come true. You will be different.

I first discovered this method in Robert Fritz's book *The Path of Least Resistance*. It was a life-changing discovery for me. The core of its methodology is encapsulated in the previous chapter on problem solving. It is the mobilization and use of the enormous power of your subconscious to solve a problem or, in this case, to find a path that will lead you to your goal without fail.

If you focus on your goal and let your subconscious treat it like a problem that needs to be solved, as described in the previous chapter, then your subconscious will solve the dilemma in ways that will amaze you. It will find a path to get you to the accomplishment of your goal where previously you did not see a path. It will even find the best and most efficient path for you, which is why I call it the best-path method.

The details of the best-path method are slightly more complex than the problem-solving method alone, but it is well worth the additional study and practice. You will be empowered to make practically any goal come true. Whereas the baby-step method uses the 10 percent of our brain that is the conscious portion, the best-path method uses the other 90 percent that is the subconscious portion. That should tell you how much power you have inside you that has remained largely untapped. Learn to unleash it, sit back, and watch the spectacular results. Most importantly, you will be able to predict the future — because you'll be the one creating it. Life's unfortunate circumstances will disappear because this method will enable you to create your own circumstances.

What makes this method work is the tension that is created in your mind. When you set your subconscious in motion to solve your problem for you in the background, tension is created that will demand resolution. Achieving your goal is that resolution, so your subconscious, properly mobilized, will not quit until it resolves said tension. In other words, your mind will not quit until it reaches a point of equilibrium, which in this case is the same as the resolution or achievement of your goal — and it will get there via the most efficient path, one that only the power of your subconscious could have found.

Goal setting is a common ingredient among all successful people. Once a goal is reached, a new goal is set. The attainment of each goal, and even completing the smaller steps leading up to that goal, is a great source of satisfaction for every entrepreneur, but it is also the journey itself. The attainment of a goal is never the end. There are always higher levels of success to reach, more ambitious goals to tackle, and more to achieve. The road to success should be a never-ending road because of the joys that the journey will bring.

Consider this saying: "Find out what poor people do and then STOP doing that!" Ask a few poor people if they use to-do lists or if they set goals. I think you already know the answer. Poor people are poor because of their habits. Change their habits, and almost any poor person can become successful and even wealthy. Proper goal setting is one of those habits. As always, knowledge is the key.

"Give me a stock clerk with a goal and I'll
give you a man who will make history.
Give me a man with no goals and
I'll give you a stock clerk."
–J.C. Penney

Do Only One Thing and
Do It Really, Really Well

This lesson is about a mistake that many beginning entrepreneurs make. I discovered this during my days as a business-plan writer. When I saw someone make this mistake, I knew their business was already dead on arrival. The scenario typically went like this.

A potential new client would approach me to write a business plan for their venture so that they could go out and raise the necessary funds. I am always interested in what a new entrepreneur plans to do, so my first request is always asking them to tell me about their business.

The following is a real-life business idea that was explained to me as the venture that my potential client was contemplating. It was a unique twist on telephone calling cards that were very popular at the time. I was told how these calling cards were different from others, and I agreed. But then I was also told how many billions of dollars the telecommunications industry generated, and if my client got only half of one percent of that business, they would generate so many tens of millions of dollars in revenue. That claim was a clear danger sign to me, and I already knew what came next.

I was told how they would provide all kinds of other services in the telecom industry including voice mail, eventual landline services, ventures into the then nascent cell-phone industry, Internet services, and just about every other aspect of what was available in telecommunications. Nothing was left out. With all those different sources of income, they would eventually reach revenues in the billions — and this was their first entrepreneurial venture.

As they threw all their different visions of grandeur at me they stared me in the eye, clearly expecting to see how incredibly impressed I was with their amazing potential. But my reaction was the exact opposite. I told them they were destined to fail and that their failure would be a 100 percent certainty. Their faces went blank.

I then asked them the same question I ask anyone who presents me with such a grandiose scheme, "What do all great companies throughout history have in common?" More blank stares. I proceeded to explain.

What all great companies throughout history have in common is that they have always started with a focus on doing one thing only and doing it better than anyone else. Anyone who goes out there and tries to collect on dozens of different revenue sources simultaneously is too scattered for any of them to come to fruition. Inevitably the whole venture will fail.

Look at the early days of any successful company, such as IBM, Xerox, Apple, Microsoft, or any of hundreds of others. They all started with one product or service and positioned themselves to be unique or better in some way. This made them grow, made them profitable, and gave them the staying power to continue to dominate for many, many years.

There are no success stories that came from companies that did not follow this formula. In fact, I challenge you to name one that tried and is still around. This does not mean that a company cannot eventually have multiple sources of revenue. To do so, however, one must first succeed with one product or service, the one that creates the company's original brand, and then you can add on others.

Apple didn't come out with their computer, iPhone, AppleTV, iPod and iPad all at once. They started with one product, with single-minded focus, and made it successful before venturing toward new horizons. Even Richard Branson's Virgin Group, covering numerous different industries, started out with just one, Virgin Records, a low-priced record label. Their first release was "Tubular Bells" by Mike Oldfield in 1973, and it became a chart-topping best seller. Branson's next venture was not added until the first was successful and profitable. Now there are over 400 separate companies under his umbrella, but it happened step-by-step, never with a shotgun approach.

So whatever it is you want to do, make sure you do one thing only, but do your best to do it better than anyone else. Focus on nothing else but the success of a single product or service. Once you've arrived, you can add another. If you try to be everything to everyone right away, you'll end up with nothing. It simply doesn't work, and this is definitely one of those absolute, make-or-break lessons you simply cannot ignore.

"FOCUS stands for Follow One
Course Until Successful."

Money Magnets

"Money is usually attracted, not pursued."

–Jim Rohn

Although many businesses can be started with little capital, many entrepreneurs will have to raise money for their new venture. This is not uncommon, and it is a topic that can fill many books. We will limit our discussion, however, to fundraising's most important must-know aspect: that which attracts capital to you. This means that you can position yourself and your idea so that money comes to you rather than you having to chase it by pounding on endless doors. In other words, there are projects and entrepreneurs out there that have positioned themselves in a way where people *want* to invest in their venture. That which attracts money to your venture is called a money magnet.

"Money magnets" is a term that was coined by America's number one entrepreneurial forum CEO Space (formerly called Income Builders International or IBI). Its founder, Berny Dohrmann, is responsible for creating more millionaires in this country than any other individual. CEO Space is a magical place where dreams come true and miracles happen on an hourly basis. Several years ago I taught there on the topic of money magnets, alongside prominent instructors such as Jack Canfield, Marc Victor Hanson, Bob Proctor, John Grey, Lisa Nichols, T. Harv Ecker, and many, many more.

The topic of attracting capital via money magnets has always been one I believed in deeply as I have made it work for me on several occasions. Just like you can attract success rather than having to chase it, you can attract money. I perfected the system to such a degree that people actually came to me to ask me if they could invest in my project. I was told on more than one occasion that it was privilege to be a financial participant in my company. I want to teach you to be able to do the same.

We will discuss the most prominent capital-attracting devices, including one that soars highest above them all, and also a few that repel capital.

The topic of money magnets is not just for those who need an outside investment. It is the concept of attraction, just like in the law of attraction, that is the major lesson. It is the difference between marketing and selling. Effective marketing brings customers to you. Just like I have done, you can get them to knock on your door rather than the other way around.

In the end you'll find that you actually needed only one or two money magnets to attract the capital you need because each investor will respond to and be motivated by only one or two of them, depending on where their priorities lie. However, since you don't know which ones they will respond to, it makes sense to pay attention to all of them. The ones your investor will respond to are the ones that in their eyes are the most compelling and irresistible. But this differs from one investor to another.

It also pays to put yourself in your investor's shoes. What would it take to make you invest in your project — or any other project for that matter? These are probably the money magnets you should focus on most.

During the time you are raising capital, you must put yourself in the frame of mind that raising capital is your current business, and you must therefore treat it like a business. Take a very organized approach. You can even create a capital team that will bring leads for potential investors to you. Remember that if you need capital, then that capital is the fuel that will help you make your dream come true. Without it, your dream will remain just a dream.

Here is a list of some of the major money magnets.

Concept – Your concept is your business idea. It includes your vision, which shows who you are and what kind of company you want to create. Is it one that helps others or the environment, or is it something destructive? In today's world it pays to help our fellow man or our planet in some way as we have become much more socially conscious than we were thirty years ago.

Your concept should also describe a problem you are solving and how your company will be the solution to that problem. In fact, this is also the best way to come up with a great concept. Isolate a problem that you have in your life that other people likely also have, and come up with a solution to your problem. Many great business ideas have been generated from this process. What problem are you the solution to, and how many other people have that same problem? This will be the size of your potential market.

Passion – This book contains an entire chapter on the power of passion because it is one of the most important forces guaranteeing your success. Allow me to relay a story to you from my own life to show you what passion can do all on its own.

The first time I needed capital to start a business I was still quite inexperienced with a very limited entrepreneurial background. The business I wanted to get into was a variation on a mail-order sweepstakes business, one that I knew little to nothing about. It was one that I saw a few other companies participating in with huge success. My confidence in being able to duplicate what they were doing was absolute, and I was excited beyond words about the idea. As a result, a friend introduced me to a gentleman who would have been a key vendor in this business, and I knew he would welcome another large customer, especially since it could be one that he would have a close involvement in, that is, if he invested in me.

I basically explained to him how I could do the same thing these other companies were doing, some of whom were also his customers, and bring him a huge amount of business as a result. It was obvious that I had neither background in the business nor much experience in running any kind of business. I was only in my mid to late twenties. What I did have though was overflowing passion and unlimited confidence in myself, which showed in every word that I spoke. My excitement knew no limits. Thus I secured a $50,000 investment to run a test to see how I would do.

The test failed. We barely broke even. I went back to my investor and explained with equal passion and confidence that the reason the test failed was that our costs were too high. We needed to mail in greater volumes to use economies of scale to reduce our unit cost. Then we would be profitable.

My investor pledged $250,000 to try again in greater volume. This time we succeeded. The company went on to generate millions in profits for my investor, and it became my first substantial success. I attribute it solely to my passion. Without it, I would have never even been able to take the first step because the money would have been withheld. Passion became the only money magnet I had in this situation. And it obviously worked.

Presentation and Visual Aids – When raising money, you will often have to do presentations for potential investors. Your presentation includes how you present yourself, your dress, your professionalism, your confidence, etc. It may also include one or more of the following: a prototype, a video, a PowerPoint presentation or slide show, and a business plan.

Whether it's you or your display materials, the quality of your presentation matters. Remember that if you want to be a big business tomorrow, you have to start acting like one today. I learned this the hard way when it once got back to me that my business acumen was being questioned by some of my vendors because I always showed up in cowboy boots and a trench coat. Live and learn. My fashion statement was clearly a little misguided.

Business Plan – A business plan by itself will rarely raise capital, but without one it is exceedingly difficult to find investment funds. A business plan is your road map. It will show how you plan to get from now to the fulfillment of your goal.

Women know the importance of planning better than men. That's why men get lost more often, we don't ask for directions, even when we continue to drive around in circles. Investors want to know that you know the direction you're headed in and how you'll get there. That's what your business plan is for.

You build a house using a plan just like you build a business with a plan. You also raise capital with a plan. Because of their failure to plan, 90 percent of businesses fail. Don't make this same mistake because if you fail to plan, then you plan to fail. Another way to look at it is like this: if you don't know where you are going, how are you going to get there?

Business planning is definitely a topic I know a lot about as I wrote business plans for a living for several years. The first aspect of writing a business plan is to determine who should write it. If you don't have any experience in this endeavor, then you probably should hire someone. I also do not recommend using an off-the-shelf template program as these are often too generic, which will be evident in the final product. You should also not get hung up on someone "being a professional." The number of plans someone has written is not necessarily the deciding criteria. They could all be terrible. Remember — professionals built the Titanic. Amateurs built the Ark.

When interviewing potential business-plan writers, I recommend paying attention to one overriding factor. If a business-plan writer tells you that he'll take all the information you have for him and then write your plan, definitely reject him. There's a missing key ingredient in this scenario.

A good business-plan writer will provide you with an extensive questionnaire, whether it's in written form or done orally, that forces you to dissect and engineer every aspect of your business to make sure everything has been considered and that it makes sense from all angles. This is a vital exercise for you that will not only make your business plan much better, but it will also help you to fine-tune your concept. Pick someone you resonate with who knows the importance of asking you lots of questions.

All business plans have similar components, including a one- or two-page executive summary, which is a quick, compelling overview of the entire plan. Some investors will read just the executive summary and only browse through the rest, so don't be surprised if that happens. This is where your language becomes most important, in the executive summary, as we'll discuss shortly.

The other major components of a business plan are as follows.

Your *Operational Plan* is an explanation of your path from now to where you want to go. It includes your concept and a step-by-step plan toward success. Investors want to know that your idea has been properly thought through. They want to see that you will plan your work and then work your plan. This doesn't mean that your plan should be rigid and adhered to in its original iteration no matter what. It can change and evolve as conditions change, or you may simply improve the plan over time as new ideas come to mind. In fact, if it doesn't evolve as you move forward, then there's probably something wrong. Remember, the only permanent thing we have is change.

Your *Marketing Plan* will show the demand for your product or service and how you plan to get it into the marketplace. A feasibility study will show an analysis of those issues to show the viability of your product or service. It may also detail the competitive advantages of your idea and how you plan to deal with your competition. Note that some marketing plans are written by a different individual or company from the one who writes your business plan because marketing is a very specialized field that sometimes requires a separate expert.

Your *Financial Plan* will show your projected revenues, expenses, cash-flow requirements, profit projections, etc. It is the numbers portion of the plan that supports your idea. It is supremely important for your financial plan to tell the same story as the rest of your plan.

Then there's your *Team*. Every business plan has a section showing the bios or resumes of the company's team members. This topic will get its own section toward the end of this chapter. You'll see why when you get to it, but here's a not so subtle hint: it's more important than all the others combined by a factor of a thousand.

Lastly, your *Capital Plan* will tell your investors how they will be rewarded for their participation. In essence it is your marketing plan to your investors.

Legal Compliance – Your legal compliance is another area where investors want to see that you've done your homework. Again, it is not something that attracts capital by itself, but without it you won't get anyone to invest. It involves the type of legal entity you are starting, such as an S-corporation, a C-corporation, or an LLC, and why you chose that type of entity. Furthermore, there are numerous laws governing the raising of investor money, which may differ from state to state, so you should get competent legal advice in this area. These laws involve the net worth or income of your potential investors, how many investors you may have, and the documentation required to raise funds, such as a Subscription Agreement and a Private Placement Memorandum (PPM). These laws are also evolving regularly. The most recent development has been the availability of crowd funding, which didn't even exist just a few years ago.

Intellectual Property – This includes patents, trademarks, licenses, trade secrets, and new technologies, all of which can be extremely valuable. If you have obtained a patent on a unique new product, for example, and your feasibility study shows it to have a very viable and prosperous future in the marketplace, you have in essence secured yourself a monopoly. This can make money fly your way with investors practically demanding to participate. Likewise, if you have an exclusive license to market a product belonging to another company, then you have similarly secured yourself a monopoly in that field. Monopolies can be so valuable that they are almost like a license to print money.

Strategic Alliances, Letters of Endorsement, and Letters of Intent – These are all items that show that you already have business waiting for you, such as a letter of intent, or that others believe in your idea also, such as an endorsement letter. Needless to say, an endorsement letter from your mom is not as valuable as an endorsement letter from Richard Branson.

Amount You Invested of Your Own Money – This one should be obvious. In essence it shows that you've put your money where your mouth is. You believe in your product or idea and are willing to put your own money on the line. It also shows you won't quit and walk away if difficulties arise. It gives your potential investors a lot of security and comfort knowing that your money will be at risk as much as theirs, especially if you show that their funds will be repaid before yours.

Language – The right language can get you almost anything. What you say and how you say it matters infinitely more than most people are aware of. And most people screw this up royally by using very abstract language. Your language must be concrete and to the point. The best way to explain the difference is this: abstract is when you think you just said something profound and the person you are talking to has a blank stare.

Say everything in plain language. Say it as it is. If you're going to build a lunar colony for vegetarians, then just say so. Being a good wordsmith is not that difficult. It starts with simple, honest, and straightforward language.

Here is an example to illustrate my point. Determine which is more compelling, the first presentation or the second.

"This diverse team of channel partners was designed and implemented by a dedicated group with the purpose being to peak efficiencies of each individual enterprise member by allowing a broader range of core competencies in the high-tech industry to be bundled together to create an overall better competitive model far surpassing similar organizations in the marketplace."

Can you imagine having to read a thirty-page business plan using that kind of abstract language? You'll want to shoot yourself by the time you get to the end, yet that is the type of language many people use to try to impress. It does exactly the opposite.

Now here is an example of clean, crisp, concise, compelling language. This is the unique selling proposition (USP) of an engineering firm that specializes in creating prototypes for new inventions.

"Our guarantee is simple. If you can conceive it, we can achieve it — from napkin drawing to reality in three months or less. We will do it within budget, better than what you ordered, on time, every time."

The right language is definitely a money magnet. As previously mentioned, one area where crisp, concise language is vitally important is in your executive summary, which needs to be brief, compelling, and to the point.

YOU and Your Team – As promised, here is the section on team. You are obviously the key member of your team; therefore, your number-one money magnet is YOU. Once your potential investors get to know you, they will know your level of passion, your knowledge, persistence, resume, character, expertise, humanity, professionalism, and integrity. Nothing beats these when it comes to attracting capital. If you remember the Bill Gates story I told you in the chapter titled "Teamwork Makes the Dream Work," then you remember that ultimately investors do not put their money into projects but into people. The right people can make almost anything work. As I already told you, good ideas are a dime a dozen. It is the people who know how to turn them into reality that are priceless.

Your team contributes substantially in this area, especially if you have some shortcomings, such as in your entrepreneurial experience and past successes. There are several types of teams you may consider cultivating and then adding into your business plan's section on team. The more experienced and recognized these individuals are, the more credibility they will lend to your project.

Your *management team* consists of the people running the company. Their experience will greatly affect how investors view the potential of your venture.

Your *legal team* is there to keep you out of trouble and will show that you're not neglecting legal compliance issues, both in the area of running your company and also in raising capital.

Your *advisory team* can be a group of individuals acting as your mentors. They may have their own companies and are not actively involved in yours. They are just there to give you advice. Obviously they have to consent to being your advisor, and the more experienced and recognized they are, the more they'll add to your ability to impress your potential investors.

Your *executive team* consists of the individuals making the major decisions and guiding your company. This is an area where you have to exert great wisdom. Don't make yourself the chief financial officer if you have no accounting experience. A little humility will go a long way here. Pick people who are fully qualified to occupy the positions they are being put into.

Money Repellents – Lastly I'd like to discuss a couple items that will make money stay away from you. Failing to follow my advice on anything in this chapter on money magnets can be a deterrent to an investor wanting to participate, such as using abstract language to try to impress your audience. It simply won't work, and often you'll never even find out why the money is not being offered. But there's more.

There are two money repellents that work like poison to keep money away from you no matter how hard you try. They are need and greed. During my business plan writing career, I saw attempts to raise money primarily to cover one's primary expenses, that is, money that was not designated to be used in the company being founded but the recipient's living expenses. The first $10,000 to $20,000 was designated for such items as personal rent and other bills before anything would go toward the business. How would you react to such an offer if you were the potential investor and it was your money? If the aspiring entrepreneur can't even cover his or her own basic lifestyle, how are they going to manage your funds and build a successful company?

I have also seen financial plans with exorbitant and unrealistic executive salaries. I have even seen line items in the list of future expenditures for thousand-dollar suits for the founder. Both of these money repellents, need and greed, will be instant death to your efforts to raise funds. The funds you raise must all go to the right place, your business, not your living expenses nor your visions of instant grandeur.

The reality is that when you start a business, at first you're going to work more than what you get paid for. Later you'll get paid far more than the amount of work you have to put in. You should always keep that in mind, plan for it, and certainly don't try to change this sequence.

Here's one final piece of advice on the topic of raising capital: You should avoid directly asking a potential investor if they would like to invest. This is not a money repellant like need and greed, but your chances of them stepping forward with an offer to invest is enhanced if you ask them *who they know* who might be interested. You want them to feel like they don't want to be left out. It is the difference between being sold versus buying. We all hate to be sold, but we all love to buy. Let your prospects come to you to buy instead of making them feel like they are being sold. If they do end up "buying," then they'll be the one thanking you instead of the other way around. If in the end they don't buy and you have nothing left to lose, you can always ask them directly later and hope you get lucky.

It Is In Giving that We Receive

"You can have everything in life you want,
if you will just help other people
to get what they want."

–Zig Ziglar

This chapter is about doing the right thing in all areas of your business because it greatly enhances your chances for success from the very beginning. The world has become a much more socially conscious place compared to only a few decades ago. Today, when people make a choice between one business versus a competitor, the one who is friendlier to the environment will win. If a choice has to be made between one businessman or salesperson versus another, the one with the highest level of integrity will win. Companies who donate a small percentage of their revenues to charity also stand above those who do not. In today's world it pays to be socially conscious and responsible.

In all honesty, there are plenty of disgustingly corrupt companies and executives out there making obscene fortunes, but the world is finally waking up and fighting back. Everyone has the ability to vote with their wallet by avoiding grocery stores or restaurants that sell unhealthy garbage or companies that poison us, including ones that pollute excessively. We also have the means to make our voices heard via social media to make more people aware of the good and the bad out there. The world is changing, and those without a conscience will eventually lose. Greed, after all, is not good, despite what we may have heard from

Gordon Gekko during the 1987 movie *Wall Street*. The relentless pursuit of profit and power is what we are seeing all around us right now, but it will not last forever. In the end evil always loses.

Doing the right thing should be done for the sake of doing the right thing, but it now carries an economic incentive with it also. Look at Elon Musk's companies. He makes revolutionary electric cars that sell in the hundreds of thousands, even making his technology freely available to others. He offers an in-home battery that can store the electricity produced from solar panels and now plans to create roofs that are literally made of solar panels. His company is thriving like no other, and it is all because he genuinely wants to give us a better future. The public is responding by buying his products in vast quantities. Apple is in a similar situation. It offers design, quality, and security unlike any other company and has thereby created a fanatical following of millions of people, including myself.

Integrity is the currency of the future, and you can cash in on it now. When it comes to structuring agreements, I will only enter into a win-win agreement. I am not looking to walk away the winner because I know this will come back to haunt me later on. I would rather be known as a fair negotiator and have them come back for more later as a result. For this reason, I also refuse to do business with individuals who need to come out on top, even if that means giving up the income from such a deal. I simply choose not to out of principle. We are becoming more evolved with each year, and as a result and more often than not, the prize now goes to those who are fair and honest.

I encourage you to live by a code of ethics that you will not violate at any cost. Always be honest, respectful, on time, and do what's right for the sake of doing the right thing. *Above all, always honor the agreements that you make.* In the end our word is our most important asset. But keep one thing in mind: Integrity is something you do, not something you talk about. Over the years I have noticed that those people or companies who cannot stop telling you how much integrity they have typically have none, especially those who put the word "integrity" into their company name. A biblical principle addresses this issue: Integrity is what you do that's right when no one is looking, and if you tell, then it doesn't count. So next time you want to give a homeless person some money, how about slipping a five- or ten-dollar bill into the pocket of a homeless person while he is sleeping and therefore won't know who put it there?

In your business, choose an endeavor that benefits other people. This is no longer hard to do, and you can still make your fortune. I have always referred to this concept as compassionate capitalism, and I have made it work for me on multiple occasions. My first distinct venture into this was a concept I came up with to help needy kids around the world that had never been attempted before. I took child sponsorships like those you hear offered on TV and made them the product in a network-marketing company. This simply meant that instead of spending a certain percentage of our revenues on advertising to attract sponsors, we redirected those same dollars into the pockets of American families in the form of commissions. We paid them to find us more sponsors in standard MLM fashion. We not only supported several thousand children around the world after just one year, but we also provided a living to many families who built large organizations of distributors, thereby supporting more and more needy kids — and thereby also giving these families the means to make a real and profound difference in the world.

The best part about this entire concept and company was how my employees and I felt about how we were making a living. We absolutely loved coming to work each day, and it was an incredibly fulfilling experience. If you are interested in knowing more about this company or concept, the entire journey is detailed in the final chapter on destiny in my first *20/20 Hindsight* book.

You can do the same. Nothing creates more passion and fulfillment than helping others. You can do it profitably, and there are an endless number of ideas for you to choose from. Best of all, it gives you an advantage in the marketplace. Furthermore, if you already know your passion, I am convinced that it can be cleverly arranged to help others in some way, even if it's not immediately obvious.

A few years ago I got into the gold-buying business. We bought gold, silver, platinum, and diamonds from the general public. Although I went into the business because I have always loved precious metals, it soon became obvious that we were providing a means for thousands of families to pay rent when money ran short or even giving them the ability to buy their kids a birthday or Christmas present when their paycheck-to-paycheck lifestyle didn't allow for any luxuries. I cannot count the number of people who left our stores with tears of gratitude in their eyes because we just saved them from becoming homeless by buying their unwanted jewelry for a fair price. This is what provided us with a feeling of accomplishment, not the money we made.

The point is that any company that provides a fairly priced, quality product or service that addresses a need in the marketplace is probably helping others in some way. It doesn't always have to be a charitable organization organized as a nonprofit. There are plenty of vastly profitable companies

SIDE EFFECTS MAY INCLUDE HAPPINESS

out there doing us all a world of good. And they're the ones who are going to survive in the end.

Numerous studies have been done to determine what contributes most to our happiness. Giving and serving are always on top. So if you do something that helps others, then your happiness is enhanced. Furthermore, your increased happiness will increase your passion, which, as you have already learned, will increase your chances for greater success.

A valid final question is whether the topic covered in this chapter is truly mandatory to follow as the lessons in this book are meant to be. The answer is quick and easy. No, it is not a do-or-die situation like most of the other lessons, and it actually is possible to succeed with lapses of integrity — for now. However, I believe this is changing, and the day will come when integrity in business will become a mandatory absolute. You will not be able to thrive without it. I don't know how soon this may happen, but I believe it will happen, so why not prepare for it now? It's also the right thing to do.

Be the Wayne Gretzky of the business world. When asked why he is so much better than others at playing hockey, he responded, "I don't skate to where the puck is. I skate to where the puck is going." You can do the same. Go to where the business world is going. Do it from the beginning.

"Be the change that you wish to see in the world."
–Mahatma Gandhi

Take Action

"You don't have to be great to start,
but you have to start to be great."

–Zig Ziglar

A wise man once said (I think it was me) that there's only one way to get something done and that is to do it. This is what separates the men from the boys. The most successful entrepreneurs just go out and do it. They don't talk about it endlessly; they just do it. They don't wait until they feel the time is just right, nor do they wait until they believe that they have prepared every little detail. They know that without immediate action they will never succeed as well as they could.

This is one of those areas that I followed intuitively early on. Even when I didn't know anything about the business I was contemplating entering, as long as I was interested in it, I just went ahead and did it. I learned along the way and let nothing hold me back. The act of doing was satisfying in ways that endless planning could never be. Learning new information and skills that interested me made it even more exciting.

Here's an example from my business plan writing days that made me recognize a group of individuals who might as well have had "dead on arrival" written on the cover of their business plan. They planned endlessly. There was always one more seminar to attend, another vendor to interview, and countless (pointless) meetings to attend. They never got off the ground to start their business. They really thought that their endless planning could get them to a point of perfect preparedness, but there is no such thing because the marketplace is evolving on a daily basis. Assuming you can even get to a point where you think you have done everything to prepare, inevitably something else will come up because of a change in the marketplace. So there really is no such thing as total preparedness.

Another great way of looking at these people and their situation is a sign I once saw on a sales manager's desk that read: "Do not confuse effort with results." Wow, that says it all. I know we all know people who are endless busybodies but never really accomplish much. Maybe you've found yourself in the same predicament. If so, it's time to change.

Many of the individuals I just described ended up giving up on their project because someone else suddenly appeared from out of nowhere and did the same thing they wanted to do — and they did it without hesitation, without endless preparation, and without worry. They just made a decision and moved on it immediately.

Procrastination is probably one of the greatest success killers out there. It doesn't matter what your reasoning is — fear of failure, fear of success, doubt — it doesn't matter. Eliminate any forms of hesitation from your life completely. It never ends up with a positive outcome. Action is the key to success. Every path starts with the first step. *When* you take that first step will determine your chances for success. You don't need to be fully prepared. You don't need to know everything about your field. All you need is a strong interest in what you're doing and then you need action.

Here are a few tips on how to take action most effectively. First, to-do lists are worth their weight in gold. Make a list of things that need to be done even if it's not complete. I have used to-do lists since childhood. I have them on my phone, on my computer, and on paper. The act of checking off completed items is a daily source of satisfaction, and to-do lists keep you from forgetting things. Your brainpower is better spent on problem solving than on remembering what needs to be done, so write it down. Reviewing your list at the end of the day can help you plan your next day for maximum efficiency.

You can have multiple lists. One could be for miscellaneous items you need to do. Another may be specific to your business. Follow your intuition and structure them in a way that feels right to you. Completed items get checked off, and what's left on the list carries over into the next day.

One of the greatest little tricks I have discovered is one that makes your day brighter and keeps you from endlessly pushing some items forward. That trick is to do what you like least, first. Most of us will postpone unpleasant tasks endlessly. The problem with this, other than not getting them done, is that they also remain in the back of our mind, depressing our mood. If you do it early in your day and you have nothing but tasks left that you enjoy completing, your day will be infinitely brighter. Trust me on this and try it. Just get the unpleasant stuff out of the way.

There are seven days in your week. "Someday" is not one of them.

This technique also saves time. Every time you shuffle the unpleasant items on your list forward, you waste time. Just thinking about them over and over again wastes time, so get them out of the way. After a few days of following this method, things will suddenly appear less unpleasant, and you will feel less hesitation to complete any items on your list. The bottom line to this trick is that it works.

As you have possibly repeatedly read in this and other books of mine, I always jump right in, usually without even knowing much about a business. If a mistake happens, it is usually minor and of little consequence. I have actually come to the conclusion that there are no mistakes, only lessons. My mistakes have taught me the most valuable lessons of all.

Action brings satisfaction, and ultimately that's what we're after because action and satisfaction in a field we may be passionate about bring fulfillment. And fulfillment is the definition of success.

"You are what you do, not what you say you'll do."

–C.G. Jung

Conclusion

In conclusion, I would like to answer a question and address a common misconception about risk taking. Most people are under the impression that entrepreneurs always put everything on the line and thereby put themselves into a do-or-die situation. They give up their job, put every dime they own at risk, and either succeed dramatically or end up on the streets. This scenario is entirely plausible, and some do follow this formula, especially since some people believe that if you put everything on the line, your chances for success are greatly enhanced. They believe this because you really leave yourself no choice in this scenario but to succeed because if you don't, you really could end up on the streets.

I do not believe in this strategy, nor have I ever followed it. I also don't believe it to be a common practice for most entrepreneurs. In my opinion entrepreneurs are not always the all-or-nothing risk takers people assume they are. We do take risks, but they are calculated risks. When I started my first business, a delivery service for fast-food restaurants, it operated seven days a week from 6:00 p.m. to midnight, but during the day I had a job to support myself. I was still new to the world of entrepreneurism and hadn't yet learned the lessons for certain success. Even later during my career I never put all my financial reserves on the line. I always worked with a backup plan in case things didn't work out as planned.

I urge you to do the same. Don't risk your entire existence. It is just not necessary. You can start small or you can start part-time until you build up enough confidence to go all-out. Practice makes perfect, so practice the lessons in this book first until they become a part of you. That is, you want to practice them until they become habits.

You don't need to invest all your savings. Always remain prepared for a rainy day. If you want to go all-out right away, that is your choice, and I know some people who do so with great success. But that is your choice, not my advice. My advice is to control your level of risk so that your livelihood, as well as your family's, is not suddenly in peril. Calculated risk taking has always worked well for me. There's no reason it shouldn't keep you sleeping better at night also.

I would like to also encourage you to enjoy the journey. It is not just about your destination, which you probably think is success and wealth. But enjoying the journey is in itself success. In fact, this is another ingredient for creating a thriving business. If you enjoy the process of building your business, the process of being an entrepreneur, then your chances for success are that much more likely. It is definitely a common ingredient among successful entrepreneurs. They love not just the field they are in but also their entire world of being in business.

Successful entrepreneurs have developed a passion for building businesses, regardless of what industries they may be working in. They enjoy the act of creation and building. They enjoy the challenges and finding solutions to problems. They enjoy working with people, their employees as well as vendors and even competitors. They love helping others with their business endeavors. The business world is full of intrigue, change, and strategy. It only gets boring if you stop growing and innovating, which you should never do anyway as stagnation eventually leads to disaster.

The process should be fun and you can make it such. It is entirely your choice. But again, keep in mind that if the process is not something you learn to love, then your chances for success diminish dramatically. Once again, it is passion that leads to accomplishments. Lack of passion makes success stay a distant dream.

I would also like to point out one more time that the lessons in this book are largely required lessons for success, not technical skills. They are life skills, character traits, attitude, and general lessons transferrable to any type of business. These are the ones that make or break you.

Technical skills, such as what kind of business structure to choose or learning how to use an accounting program, are ones you can learn by asking what choices other businesspeople have made. For example, if you want to learn what accounting program is best for you, just ask a few people in similar industries with businesses of similar size what they use. Ask several people and then make your choice. I typically use QuickBooks for virtually any endeavor. If you make a mistake in your choice, then it is typically something that can be corrected without much upset later.

Technical issues are just not nearly as important as your passion, your determination, your integrity, your motivation, your problem-solving skills, your attitude toward wealth and success, and your understanding of the laws that govern your behavior, such as the law of abundance. I don't mean to belittle technical skills, such as properly structuring a partnership, asset protection, or effectively managing people. That's why I cover many of these lessons I learned over the years in my other books. But this book is only about those lessons that are absolute requirements, without which success becomes nearly impossible. Learn them well, and they will also make success a predetermined certainty for you. If you want to learn the other lessons right away so that you avoid bumps in the road early on, you can. Absorbing those other lessons will not overload you. They will only make your fortress even more secure.

If I can do it, so can you. I did not have any special privilege growing up. I simply enjoyed learning, became a lifelong student of personal growth and motivational materials, and discovered early on the benefit of following your passions. Anthony Robbins said that passion is the genesis of genius. This means that by following your passion, you too can unleash genius you didn't even know you had.

I started small, endured a few failures, and learned to embrace the lessons I learned from challenges and mistakes. I recognized that temporary defeat never needs to become permanent failure. Setbacks are just more valuable lessons we should be thankful for.

There is nothing in my past that made my chances for success any greater than what you have at your disposal. So rest assured that you have everything you need at your fingertips right now to succeed. You truly can escape your nine-to-five miseries and live your life's passion. You can realize all your dreams, and best of all, you can find and follow your purpose. By doing so you will discover your innate talents. These are your gifts from God. What you do with them is your gift back to God.

> *"That some should be rich shows that*
> *others may become rich."*
>
> –Abraham Lincoln

Summary List

What follows is a summary of all the lessons in this book. Please do not make the mistake of reading this list without first reading the full chapters in this book as each lesson requires supporting details to fully understand the lesson. There's always more to it than meets the eye. Without its supporting information, this summary list would be all but useless to most people who are just starting out.

The following list should serve as a checklist for you to see if you have not yet fully integrated any of the lessons. If so, go back and reread the relevant chapter(s) again until you do. This list can also serve as a reminder list that you can refer back to occasionally. Please note that it is not necessarily a lesson-per-chapter list as there are some lessons that are woven throughout the book without each lesson having its own separate chapter.

Here are the major lessons:

- Money alone does not make you happy, successful, or grant you fulfillment. Money is merely a by-product. Success comes from doing something you love, and the money will typically follow automatically. If not, there are ways of making it follow. So get rid of the thought that money alone will make you happy, or your chances for true success will be diminished dramatically. Money alone will not make you happy as witnessed by the many miserable rich people out there who are not living their true passion or purpose.

- Success can become a predetermined certainty for you. It comes from learning the right lessons, following them, and not neglecting any of them. Those key lessons are transferrable to any business as they are not technical skills specific to a certain type of business. The important lessons are universal lessons. Some could even be called life lessons. They apply here as well as in any other country in the free world.

- The lessons you need to learn to become successful must come from someone who has been there and done that. They can come directly from a mentor who guides you or from a book such as this one written by someone who has learned from experience the important lessons that will make or break you. This is where most of us started out on the wrong foot. We got all our advice for our career choices from people who have never experienced real success for themselves. This has guided us into a life of mediocrity and conformity where we are not following our passions.

- Persistence is a most powerful tool that can overcome almost any obstacle. It can be your ace in the hole that will outshine any other. Develop a "failure is not an option" attitude, and nothing will be able to stand in your way. Press on, even when things look bleak, as there is always a solution for every problem to get you back on track. Giving up is what will make you fail. Persisting no matter what is what will make you succeed.

- You absolutely must have the right mind-set toward success. If you believe that most wealthy people became that way dishonestly, then you will fail in your own entrepreneurial endeavor. If you have a dependence or welfare mentality and blame everything wrong in your life on someone else, you will likewise fail. If you think the world owes you something, then your chances for success will also be close to zero. Successful people take responsibility for everything in their lives, good and bad. They know that their hardships, challenges, and mistakes were merely lessons they had to learn, and they are grateful for them for that reason.

- Our thoughts and emotions create our external reality. Happiness and success come from the inside and then manifest in our outside world, not the other way around. Whatever we put out will come back to us, as in what goes around comes around, good and bad. This is the law of abundance. Knowing this allows you to create whatever you want for your future by laying the groundwork now. You are literally the co-creator of your external reality and your life. Use this knowledge wisely by putting out positive thoughts and emotions so you attract the right kind of future.

- Doing something you are passionate about is your greatest success and wealth-building secret. If you love what you do, then you have the motivation to get up each day because you'll look forward to the work you do. It also keeps you from quitting because you're not going to give up that which you love doing. And it allows you to quickly learn all you need to learn so that you can become an expert in your field. Learning something you are not interested in is extremely difficult.

- Passion leads to motivation, and being properly motivated is the key to your success, wealth, and happiness. There are three kinds of motivation. From least to most powerful, the first is external, such as from books, audio programs, or seminars. Then there is internalized motivation (external that becomes internal), such as an interest that becomes a passion. Finally, there is internal motivation, which comes from our core values and core desires. It is the most powerful. These are part of who we are and cannot be ignored. They are our number-one driving force. Ideally our core values and core desires should be incorporated into our business ventures. It will pay tremendous dividends to find out exactly where your primary motivations lie. Most people don't know, but a few simple exercises can help you find out. They are described in the chapter on motivation.

- All three sources of motivation can be extremely useful in raising our chances for success. But what most people don't know is that external motivation, such as from books, audio recordings, and seminars, must be repeated almost daily or it won't last. To be a true student of personal development, you must feed yourself with personal growth information on an almost daily basis. This is the only way to effectively tap into the power of external motivation.

- No one becomes successful alone. We have mentors that teach us, team members to brainstorm with, employees who must support our vision, and even customers who must buy our product or service for us to succeed. The team we surround ourselves with is infinitely more important than our idea. An experienced team can turn a mediocre idea into a financial powerhouse, but a mediocre team may destroy even the best of ideas because they don't know what they are doing. Ideas, even great ideas, are a dime a dozen, but the people who turn them into reality are priceless.

- If you are going to have a partner, your partnership must be structured correctly, otherwise your company will probably not make it. It is disagreements over the small issues that create conflict because emotion and ego will get in the way. For this reason, you must structure your company into departments where each department has a leader with the final say-so in case there is a disagreement. You can still make decisions together and share everything with nothing but good intentions, but when an inevitable disagreement does arise, someone needs to have veto power. It is the only way. Equality may sound good, but it can lead to the total annihilation of your business. Human nature is the culprit when that happens. Every department must have a boss. Period.

- Problems, challenges, setbacks, and roadblocks are a normal part of being an entrepreneur. Fortunately, every dilemma has a solution. To find that solution you can let your subconscious do the work for you. Your subconscious is infinitely more powerful than your conscious mind and has the ability to perform miracles on a daily basis. Learn to mobilize your subconscious to solve your problems for you and you'll become unstoppable. Do this by focusing on solving the problem consciously, almost until exhaustion, and then letting go. If the solution does not present itself, then forget about the issue and your subconscious will automatically continue working on your dilemma. Then, within the next few days the answer will appear out of the blue, sometimes even in the middle of the night.

- Goal setting is a discipline that anyone who wants to become successful must practice and should learn to master. Setting a deadline for your goals differentiates them from mere dreams or fantasies. If you learn the right goal-setting techniques, then even goals that seem virtually unachievable can be turned into reality. A conscious method for achieving a goal involves breaking it down into numerous baby steps, each easily achievable. This is for goals where you know the path that will lead you to the finish line. For those goals where the path is not known, you can use your subconscious mind to create the path for you. This best-path method is similar to the problem-solving technique where you mobilize your subconscious to do what the conscious mind cannot.

- Do one thing and do it better than anyone else. All great companies became great because of their single-minded focus on one product or service. Companies that try to be everything to everyone with dozens of revenue sources almost always fail. Additional products and services can be added later, once the first is successful, but never take a shotgun approach. Furthermore, because our world is becoming increasingly socially conscious, your product or service should benefit society in some way. Do something worthwhile that solves a problem, fulfills a need, and helps as many people as possible. It is the way of the future.

- If you need to raise money for your venture, then learn to attract capital rather than going out soliciting for money. It is the difference between buying and selling. We all hate to be sold, but we all love to buy. It is possible to position your company so that investors want to invest because it all looks so incredibly compelling. Get them to want to buy. Things that attract capital are called "money magnets" and can include your presentation, the language you use, your business plan, your idea and vision, and many more. But your number-one money magnet is a qualified, experienced team. Investors invest in people, not in ideas.

- If you are raising capital, beware of that which repels money, need and greed. Don't raise money to cover your personal expenses, and don't even think about paying yourself a lot during the start-up stages. If any of these appear in your financial projections, you can be sure that you will not find the funding you seek.

- Do the right thing. Live your life with integrity and build your business according to the same principles. This is the foundation you are laying for what will be returned to you later. Do it for this reason but also because it's the right thing to do. Make only win-win agreements, and create a code of ethics that you will live and work by. Do not deviate from it, and only do business with those people who are like-minded and return the same courtesies to you. Above all, always stand by the agreements you make.

- Do not confuse effort with results. There are countless great ideas that never get launched because their founders were spinning their wheels on endless preparation. Just go out there and do it. Take action. There is no greater deterrent to achieving your goals than procrastination or being a busybody. Don't think that you need to prepare until everything looks perfect. There is no such thing because the marketplace is changing on a daily basis. Just get out there and do it. You can learn much of what you need to know along the way. You can also adapt to prevailing market conditions along the way. When something clearly does need to get done, do it right away without postponing it, especially if it's something you don't particularly enjoy doing. Get that out of the way first. Otherwise, the act of shuffling things around only wastes time.

- **Most important:** Enjoy the journey!

About the Author

For 25 years, Parviz Firouzgar has been the owner of numerous multi-million dollar companies in a variety of industries, sometimes running several ventures simultaneously, both for profit and nonprofit entities. Some of Parviz's companies involved the use of investor funds of up to several million dollars. As mentioned, one investor walked away with $1.7 million in one year as a result of his confidence in the author's abilities when Parviz was just in his 20's.

Parviz founded a mortgage company and employed over 500 loan officers. He wrote business plans for startup companies that helped them raise many millions in startup capital. After he discovered a new way of raising funds, he expanded into the charitable arena. Within one year, his company was supporting 2,300 needy children around the world, providing all their food, clothing, and education.

Parviz has been in the direct mail and sweepstakes business, mailing so many millions of pieces of mail each month that his local post office had to expand their operations. Most recently, he has been in the precious metals and diamond business, including owning a gold mine.

Parviz was a radio talk show host and a long time instructor for Income Builders International (IBI), now called CEO Space, an entrepreneurial forum with internationally recognized instructors, such as: Jack Canfield, Mark Victor Hansen, Bob Proctor, T. Harv Eker, John Gray, and Lisa Nichols.

Raised in Europe, Parviz speaks four languages. He has been accepted for membership in Mensa and Intertel, both high I.Q. societies.

Connect with Parviz Firouzgar

Facebook: www.facebook.com/pfirouzgar

LinkedIn: www.linkedin.com/pub/parviz-firouzgar/ b6/8b4/91

Twitter: @ParvizFirouzgar

Email: Parviz@ParvizFirouzgar.com

Websites: www.ParvizFirouzgar.com
www.SuccessLibrary.com

Other Books by Parviz Firouzgar

20/20 Hindsight

20/20 Hindsight - Additional Lessons

The Secrets of Wealth

Motivation - Your Master Key to Success and Riches

In Gratitude to You

I would be so grateful if you could take a minute or two to share what you loved about this book and provide an honest review on our Amazon sales page.

21337874R00078

Printed in Great Britain
by Amazon